HOW TO STAY ALIVE
ALL YOUR LIFE

"Whatsoever things are true,
whatsoever things are honest,
whatsoever things are just,
whatsoever things are pure,
whatsoever things are lovely,
whatsoever things are of good report;
if there be any virtue,
and if there be any praise,
think on these things."

PHILIPPIANS 4:8.

HOW TO STAY ALIVE
ALL YOUR LIFE

by

C. W. FRANKE

ZONDERVAN PUBLISHING HOUSE
Grand Rapids, Michigan

Dedicated to my three sons

DAVID, DWIGHT and DANIEL

with the prayer that they will always live the
cheerful, victorious, Christian life as
joyfully as they now want to play.

FOREWORD

The author of this book is a man whom I have come to know and respect as a fellow Christian. As an active and leading pastor in the area which I represent in the United States Congress, we share some common concerns regarding the role of the Christian in public affairs. Under his gifted leadership the people of his parish have manifested a deep and abiding interest in governmental affairs. He himself has served his community as Director of a Family Service Speakers' Bureau. As a member of the Editorial Board of one of his denominational newspapers and as a President of the Rockford, Illinois Ministerial Association, the impact of his ministry has been felt far beyond the boundary lines of his church parish.

His book, *How to Stay Alive All Your Life*, is thus a reflection of his own vibrant, purposeful and constructive ministry. It presents a challenge to those who will read it to live the strenuous life without experiencing the hypertensions so common to modern society. It does so by presenting a message that shows how by living our lives on a higher spiritual plane we discover a new meaning and relevance in our Christian faith.

—JOHN B. ANDERSON
United States Congressman
Illinois, 16th District

PREFACE

The story is told about a little girl stroking the face of a donkey, and then saying: "My, but he must be a nice Christian; he has such a long face."

Somehow too much of the solemn, long-faced approach to the Christian faith has been communicated. No wonder it is difficult for the church to hold the youth.

For a long time I have been concerned about the average church member's religion being *dull habit* and not enough *dynamic hilarity*. A keen observer in church one Sunday said he never saw so many solemn faces as the congregation sang, "Joyful, Joyful, We Adore Thee." We can never convince many that we have the joy of God's presence *inside* when we look so mournfully downhearted on the *outside*. If that is having the "Joy, Joy, Joy, Joy Down in Our Hearts," people will not want it.

In these chapters, it is my purpose to help the faithful and the seeking to know that they can live for God, behave themselves, and have fun — enjoy every moment of life. The essential thoughts in these chapters and many of the illustrations have been given in sermons from my own pulpit. Many different people have come to me again and again, both in the hour of crisis and in the gaiety of a social occasion to recall one or more of the cheerful stories and illustrations that came to them, "just at the time I needed it most." As I try to do in all my sermons and writings, I have sought to lift from life, problems and questions, apply to them the cheerful, uplifting teachings and power of the Master and put them into chapters that will fit back into life—your life.

It is my hope and prayer that young people and adults, upon digesting these chapters, will see the Christian faith truly as it is— cheerful, optimistic, dynamic—and upon giving themselves to it, will find the good life that enables a person truly to stay alive as long as he lives. If this is accomplished in a few lives, I shall be more than repaid for whatever time and effort have gone into the writing of these chapters.

—C. W. Franke

Rockford, Illinois

CONTENTS

Foreword
Preface

HOW TO STAY ALIVE
ALL YOUR LIFE

1. THE POWER OF THE MIND OVER THE BODY

"Finally, brethren, whatsoever things are true, whatsoever things are honest, whatsoever things are just, whatsoever things are pure, whatsoever things are lovely, whatsoever things are of good report . . . think on these things"   *(Philippians 4:8).*

SOMEONE HAS SAID: "WE ARE LOOKING FOR BETTER METHODS; God is looking for better people." This book, thoughtfully read, will help you become that "better person" for whom God is looking, one who has given his heart and life to Christ and accepted Him as Lord and Saviour. Through these pages, I want to share with you three things that will help bring to you the abundant life for which you have been longing. They are: the power and guidance of God as revealed to us in the Scriptures; examples of how Twentieth Century man is finding these God-given principles to be true, practical and workable; and a lively sense of humor.

Basic to the abundant life is the power of the mind over the body and all of life. A busy man arrived home very late one night, and as he went up the stairs his son heard his footsteps and called to him, asking him to come into his room for a moment. The father sat on the edge of the boy's bed. The boy asked: "Dad, are two heads better than one?" "I guess they are," said the father. To this the boy replied: "Then why doesn't your head help my head with its lessons?"

Have you ever tried that with all its potential and power and guidance in your relationship to God? We have not only our own brain, but we have the mind of God to help us as we face life and all its woe. "Whatsoever things are true . . . honest . . . just . . . pure . . . lovely . . . of good report . . . think on these things." "Have this mind in you, which was also in Jesus Christ" (Philippians 2:5 ASV). When we have that, we have power within us that will produce victory, health and happiness. Our happiness or misery is pretty much the product of our thoughts. Most people agree that generally we tend to become that which we wish to become, and our habits and way of living correspond to our thought pattern.

There is a story from the past that describes very well this power of the mind over the body. Long before the death of Henry Irving, his doctor had cautioned him against playing his famous part in *The Bells,* because of the immense strain on his heart. Ellen Terry, his leading woman for many years, says in her biography of him:

"Every time he heard the sound of bells, the throbbing of his heart must have nearly killed him. He used always to turn quite white — there was no trick about it. It was imagination acting physically on the body.

"His death as Matthias — the death of a strong, robust man — was different from all his other stage deaths. He did, really, almost die — he imagined death with such horrible intensity. His eyes would disappear upward, his face grow gray, his limbs cold.

"No wonder then, that the first time the Wolverhampton doctor's warning was disregarded, and Henry played 'The Bells' at Bradford, his heart could not stand the strain. Within twenty-four hours of his last death as 'Matthias,' he was dead."

His doctors said that this man, who had so dramatically played this part for one hundred and fifty nights, was undoubtedly dying through the entire performance. Yet, so braced up and stimulated was he by his great enthusiasm that he actually held death away for a time. One can see so much in the whole incident that would speak of the power of the mind over the body.

We have learned in recent years that it is a common experience for a person to be cured for a time and completely forget aches and pains under the stimulus of ambition and the brain-quickening influence of a time of need. When my father died, my mother and sister and I were ill. Only my father was well at the time, but a sudden heart attack took his life. Under the shock of that experience and the need for us to meet the hour with which we had been matched, we forgot about being ill and were well.

I read the other day about a man who had been wounded by a gun shot. Everyone was sure the bullet had passed through his body. Upon hearing this he fainted and fell over as though dead. He was rushed to the hospital and placed on the operating table. The doctor soon found that it was only a shallow flesh wound. The bullet had never entered his body. When the man heard the good news, he got up, smiled, dressed, and went away as if nothing had happened. Because of what his mind had thought, he had been frightened nearly to death. Such is the power of mind over the body.

In the pages that follow, we discuss how mental attitudes and mind conditions register a dynamic impact upon the body and all of life.

The Bible, in speaking of man says: "As he thinketh in his heart [or mind] so is he" (Proverbs 23:7).

I.

We have not, even now, come to know what we can bear and what we can do as a result of the power of mind over body. Every time we are put to the test we find it is tremendous. The astronauts have certainly proven this to us. The brain washing of recent years has demonstrated this truth, also.

When the automobile was invented, some people said they would never make them to go over forty miles an hour because such speed would crush the body. Now the body can be trained to stand speeds up to thousands of miles per hour and gravitational forces up to eleven times the weight of one's body. A great amount of this training involves the training of the mind to tell the body that it can be done. We do not yet know what can be done in the area of the power of mind over body.

We have, however, known for some time that there is a mammoth power here which can be put to work. As a boy, I was deathly afraid of hawks. One day, when one swooped down near me, I rushed to the house, and, in doing so, jumped a fence that I could never have jumped otherwise. A person who shrinks from the prick of a pin under ordinary circumstances can, by preparing himself mentally for it, endure without an anesthetic the pulling of a tooth or the cutting of flesh if necessary. There are records of people, far from civilization, who have endured quite well the amputation of an arm or leg without the aid of pain killers, simply because they knew it had to be done if they were to live. I have often heard of a tractor or heavy machine falling on a man, and only a few in that crisis lift it and free the injured man.

There is something within the mind of every one of us who give ourselves to Christ that can brace us up in a crisis and make us equal to the emergency. This something is the mind of God working within our minds.

"Have this mind in you, which was also in Christ Jesus" (Philippians 2:5, ASV).

On the American frontier and on many distant mission fields away from transportation and communication, people came to depend upon God so greatly — and on their own resources — that it was only on extreme occasions of emergency that a doctor was called in. The development of "miracle drugs" and modern medicine is a marvelous thing when really needed. However, one of the unfortunate things that has come with modern civilization is the killing of our faith in the power within us to resist disease. In our modern world people make great preparation for sickness. We expect it, we anticipate it, and, as a result, we have it. The ease with which we can go to the doctor and our haste to rush to the drugstore at the slightest symptom of illness tend to make us more and more dependent upon outside physical helps and less and less able to draw upon the power within to help us control illness and build bodily strength.

Proper thinking, as outlined in Philippians 4:8 will help produce sound health; on the other hand, thoughts that keep telling us that something terrible must be wrong with us encourage the inroads of disease.

The beloved Baptist preacher, James Whitcomb Brougher, Sr., said at eighty years of age: "I am always ashamed when I have a cold. I am just as ashamed of it as if I were a Christian Scientist. I am sure that if I ate properly and took the right kind of care of my body, I could keep well and free from all colds." Again, I say, we do not really know what can be accomplished through the power of God-given thoughts and the power of mind over body. We are learning more and more in this area each day.

II.

It would seem more rational, would it not, to believe that God has placed resources for health and the good life within man himself in his own mind, where they are readily available, than that He would store them exclusively outside of man in remote areas?

The testimony of Scripture and history is that man has within his mind the scepter of power and control over himself and his environment. This power becomes released in its fullness when a person comes into harmony with God. When ancient Israel turned from God it was an invitation for judgment and ruin. When these people served God, they found the good life. Outside forces, alliances with powerful nations, and earthly might could not save them. Only by determining in their minds to do what was right and serve God did they ever find peace, health and happiness.

A little girl asked her grandfather what part of the car caused the most accidents, and he replied that he did not know. She answered; "The nut that holds the wheel." That is about right. Put a better mind at the control and better things will happen. The power for control, happiness and health are within you.

Think of how rare it is that a person is ill on the day of a great occasion in which he is involved. Is not life, all of life, to be a great occasion? I think it is. Those who have been continually ill have been practically cured by having circumstances thrust upon them that forced them away from the "luxury" of just thinking about themselves, dwelling upon their troubles in self-pity. Doctors report that many of their patients have nothing wrong with them except their thoughts. One doctor whom I heard of often writes out this prescription and hands it to them: "Romans 12:2." It reads: ". . . be ye transformed by the renewing of your mind. . . ." Most of us, to achieve better control, happiness and health need to change our thought pattern more than we need some outside control, help, or force.

Think of what the world owes to that sense of "must" welling up from within that has been put to work when all outside help has been cut off, and man was forced to call on all that was within him to carry on in an unfortunate, or critical situation. Many of us recall how wartime shortages and needs forced man to look within his mind for creativity. When dyes from Germany were no longer available, we got our minds to work and developed our own. When rubber was no longer available from the islands of the seas, we developed a new kind of material that was just as good. Whether it be a nation or an individual, the real resources are in the heart and mind of man as given and put there by the Almighty God.

III.

It is this power of mind over body that causes visions to arise and visions to come true. The great King Solomon said: "Where there is no vision, the people perish" (Proverbs 29:18). He could not have been more correct. That vision comes from within and influences the whole body and all it does. Without the mind and all of its great vision, the body will perish. It will die, and the world will die with it. Every invention for our bodily comfort was once a vision — a blueprint in someone's mind. Your coat in winter and your air-conditioner in summer were first developed in someone's mind, and thus are examples of the power of mind over body.

I can hear you saying it now: "I want this business about power of mind and visions to be personal, something that can happen to me, right now, here where I live." That is exactly what God wants for you and you can have it. One of the first things you will have to do is accept the fact that Christ is a vigorous realist as well as a righteous redeemer. This is not an easy "how to do it" self-help book. It is more of a "How God will help me do it" book. Thus we will have to permit ourselves to follow His will and His thinking. Thinking on the things that God would have us think on and letting "this mind be in you which was in Christ Jesus" mean letting your mind dwell on the good things of life and the teachings of Christ until this becomes a part of you just like a piece of music that you have heard or practiced a hundred times becomes a part of you. When your mind is filled with certain tunes, you often find yourself humming and singing these tunes almost unconsciously — the power of mind over body. When your mind is filled with Christ, His life, His teachings, your mind will guide you into the good life with health and happiness.

The realistic fact is that how well we succeed will depend upon the extent to which we allow ourselves to be saturated with the good thinking of God and all His teachings in the Bible. The degree to which we have this mind of Christ will mean the difference of whether we fail or succeed, or crawl the middle way of doubt and indifference. The chapters that follow will deal with the specifics in various areas of life, on how to put to work this power of mind over body for the attainment of the good life and the sharing of it with others. Our minds and spirits should affect an atmosphere, create a climate, and thus determine to a degree the brightness or darkness of the day for others.

PRAYER: Heavenly Father, I thank Thee for giving me the opportunity to have with me this mind which was in Christ Jesus. May that mind be so working in me that I may have health, power and good cheer that will be radiant and helpful to all I meet. In His Holy Name, I pray. Amen.

2. THE POWER OF IMAGINATION

"Where there is no vision, the people perish"   *(Proverbs 29:8).*

SEVERAL YEARS AGO WHILE I WAS PASTORING A SMALL rural church, located just one mile from a busy highway, one man in the church proposed to the church officials that we erect a sign along the highway calling attention to our church, inviting tourists to attend on Sunday mornings. An official opposed it, stating that no one would see the sign and thus it would be money wasted. However, the officials voted to purchase and erect the sign. Soon after the sign was up, a carload of visitors from another state came in for church. They said: "We saw your sign." The man who had opposed the placing of the sign then said: "Now I can see it." The difference between him and the man who proposed the sign was this: The man who had made the proposal was able to see it happening in his mind as an idea. The one man had imagination. He had vision.

The story is told of a boy playing with a shaggy old dog on a street corner. An interested and kindly old man asked: "What kind of dog is he?" The boy replied: "He is a police dog." The man smiled and remarked tactfully: "He doesn't look much like one." "Oh, he is in the secret service," explained the boy. A boy's imagination had made a police dog out of a mangy old cur, as only a young lad could.

Actually, we owe the improvement of the world and the climb of civilization to the power of imagination. We would still be living in the stone age if it were not for those who, with imagination, could see something better for the future and were determined to do something about it.

The men and women who have brought us to where we are in the heights of civilization, culture and religious faith, thus rendering great service to humanity, have done so by seeing in their imagination, their vision, something infinitely better than existed in their time. They gave themselves toward making it a reality. Those who have had great vision and imagination have often challenged others to give themselves to great projects.

Let us review specifically what the power of imagination has done, and then note the power of imagination for fostering the good life of today.

I.

The power of imagination has made something better in life and society. It was because Samuel F. B. Morse saw, in his imagination, something better than the Post Office of his day for communication purposes that he was able to give the telegraph to the world. It was because Alexander Graham Bell was able to imagine something better than the telegraph that he, in 1876, gave to the world the telephone. It was because of an active imagination that Marconi in 1895, was able to give the world something even better. That something was the wireless.

Because of the musical imagination of such men as Bach, Beethoven, Mendelssohn, and Handel we have the great classic masterpieces of music. Because merchants could imagine people enjoying shopping in a leisurely fashion at one-stop shopping spots with everything within walking distance, we now have the kind of store that we have in large new shopping centers. Because the imagination of educators could see the needs of the coming generations and the possibilities for improving the human race, with expanded knowledge, we now have our schools, colleges, and technical institutes to meet the demands of a space age.

Indeed, all that we have and are, we owe to God-given imagination, vision, and inspiration. Those who see things only as they presently exist, who have no imagination for possible improvement, are the ones who usually oppose improvement measures and seek to stifle growth. When this happens a slow decay begins to set in.

This is true in our religious life as well as in the material or cultural. Because the Apostle Paul envisioned in his imagination the Christian Faith embracing the Western World, and was willing to carry that Faith westward, we have the Faith as we know it in the United States today. Because men like Martin Luther and others envisioned the common man reading his own Bible and interpreting for himself we have had men willing to sacrifice their lives to translate the Bible into the language of the man on the street. Again, history, religious and secular, has verified those old words of the Proverbs: "Where there is no vision, the people perish." Without vision, without imagination, without a living faith in Jesus Christ, people begin to die both physically and spiritually.

II.

No longer is the person of tremendous imagination considered an idle dreamer, a crank, or an impractical no-good.

I recall that many years ago my father and others would read about certain predictions in the future, and they would say: "Impossible." After the two atomic bombs were dropped on Japan, in World War II, I asked my father what he thought of it. He replied: "I will no longer say anything is impossible."

That statement reflects quite well the thinking of the people today. We are no longer saying that the things that are growing in the imaginations of our great thinkers are impossible. We are saying, as the slogan stated: "The difficult we do now; the impossible takes a little longer." The occurrence of the once impossible is becoming routine. The splitting of the atom into atomic energy, cures for diseases, pictures of the far side of the moon, flight faster than sound, transplanting of organs from one body to another to save a life, these, and other once impossibles are constantly occurring. They occur, because certain men, in their creative imagination, could see them as real possibilities.

There was a time, however, when imaginative dreamers were called impractical people. They were sometimes called cranks, or witches. Columbus was laughed at because he thought the world was round. This was fantasy of the highest sort. Many men of science, government, philosophy, and religion have been laughed at, persecuted, and even killed, because they, in their creative imaginations had visions of great things beyond their times and were willing to speak and work for the better things that finally did become a reality. Today, however, we have learned to appreciate the dreamer, the man with imagination, for he has lifted us above slavery, emancipated us from drudgery, and has given us greater insights into the nature of man, his thinking and his religious needs.

The great prophets of every age have been men of imagination, and we have learned to listen to these spokesmen with vision. Isaiah, Jeremiah, Ezekiel, and others of Old Testament days were able to envision clearly the future of Israel, and they spoke to the people, informing them that their future depended upon their loyalty to the Lord and their living righteously. However, most would not listen. Rather they preferred to listen to prophets who gave only the soothing comforting message of false security. Again, however, history has taught us to listen to the prophet with a warning. We have learned to note well the men of vision who warn of impending danger as a result of our wrong thinking and doing. The men of imagination, vision, and thought are respected among us today.

III.

It is positively recognized today that imagination is a must for the creative, good life.

This would indicate that imagination is necessary, not only in the area of scientific accomplishment, as already mentioned, but also in the areas of culture, the humanities, and our religious life. Pictures in the mind are there, not to entertain us, but to show us what can become reality.

A lively imagination is one of God's greatest gifts to mankind. A God-given imagination will present noble ideals to be achieved in life. A God-directed imagination is necessary to inspire and renew the enthusiasms of life. Someone has even said that "Imagination is the architect of the soul."

It can also be pointed out that imagination helps to develop that sense of humor so necessary to good living. It is because of a lively imagination that we are able to see the funny things about us and enjoy a humorous story. Without imagination and humor, people would become dull and pessimistic. A pessimist is a negative influence in the kingdom of God, and a drag on those who enjoy life.

Children usually have good imaginations, and this is wonderful. The mind and its imagination must be rightly directed, of course, to assure future happiness. Jesus said: "Except ye become as little children, ye shall not see the kingdom of heaven." We must have the humility, the creative imagination of a little child. Religious people with Christian vision and imagination can do for religion and the religious life what the creative artist can do for art, and what the imaginative musician can do for music. Jesus was this kind of a person. He brought to religion imagination humorously presented at times that He might drive home the point He was teaching. Consider His sayings as He taught concerning pride and hypocrisy: "Ye blind guides, which strain at a gnat, and swallow a camel."

It is obvious that Jesus was using imagination to produce a more vivid picture of what He was seeking to say. Let us direct our attention to another: "And why beholdest thou the mote that is in thy brother's eye, but considerest not the beam that is in thine own eye?" That "beam" in modern language would be a 2 x 4 piece of wood, and the "mote" would be just a speck of sawdust or something of that size. Thus, we can readily note that Jesus drew upon imagination to paint a picture with words, making an indelible impression upon His audience concerning the things about which He was teaching.

Jesus was teaching serious truth. However, He was doing it in an imaginative, even humorous way. Jesus was an imaginative, cheerful teacher. He knew what He was talking about when He said: "Except ye . . . become as little children, ye shall not enter into the kingdom of heaven." He knew that little children were cheerful, imaginative people. He knew that a small boy in a sandpile can have more enjoyment than a man with a million dollars. The small boy, with his cheerful, exuberant imagination is master of the sandpile, while the man without imagination is mastered by his million.

Imagination is vision. Imagination helps us become prophets of the possible future. It helps us to whet our ambitions. It helps us to become dissatisfied with the mediocre. It spurs us on to something infinitely better.

Without imagination, the soul, instead of growing, begins to die. Henry Ward Beecher at one time said: "Imagination is the very secret and marrow of civilization. It is the very eye of faith." No idea has ever been conceived, no piece of music has ever been composed, no poetry ever written, no painting was ever produced, no book was ever written, and no cathedral or church has ever been erected without imagination drawing invisible blueprints in the mind that later were made visible. Imagination, under the guidance of Almighty God gives us the ideals toward which men should aim and strive. Without this ideal, man ceases to grow and begins to die. When imagination is lost, enthusiasm dies; when enthusiasm dies, carelessness sets in; and when carelessness enters, one tends toward a worldliness of thought — secularization — and a drifting away from the center of the truth of God.

Someone recently wrote to one of the columnists complaining about her son and his problem of exaggeration. She was counseled that, while it is true one must come to the point where he can separate fact and fancy, she should not worry too much about this, because it is usually the normal and healthy vivid imagination of a child. He needs a vivid imagination to grow into a mature imaginative person.

The article reminded me of the story of the little boy who came running to his mother, saying: "Mama, there is a lion in the back yard." She looked out the window, and there was a very large woolly dog trimmed like a lion. She reprimanded him by saying: "Now, you knew that was a big dog and not a lion. You must go upstairs and tell God about it and ask Him to forgive you for lying." When the little fellow came down stairs, she asked if he had asked God to forgive him. He replied that he had, and that God had said to him: "That's all right. That big dog fooled Me, too." I would say that boy is going to be all right in the imagination department.

Develop a good imagination and use it constructively like Jesus did. Train the imagination so as to form the habit of producing beautiful pictures in the mind and perpetually inspiring images, and you will have a part in bringing beauty, harmony and goodness into being, all of which will enable you and all whom your life will touch to go over the heavy jolts of life with a reasonable degree of comfort, pleasure, and joy.

PRAYER: Our Almighty God, the father of all good thought, fill me with vision, inspiration, and imagination equal to the tasks before me, that I may be able to live properly, victoriously, and communicate the good word of Thy message of life and love to others. Amen.

3. THE POWER OF POSITIVE SUGGESTION

"If God be for us, who can be against us?"   (*Romans 8:31*).

MY FATHER USED TO TELL ABOUT A MAN WHO APPEARED IN
his community one day. No one had ever seen the man before. While
he was with a group of men, they heard of a prairie fire out in
the country. The fellows all rushed to the fire and extinguished it.
After they had relaxed a bit, the new man stood up and shouted:
" 'If God be for us, who can be against us?' Who can be against
us?" The man then walked away, and they never saw him again.
My father reported that the experience and statement by the strange
man impressed him and stayed in his mind. The verse impressed
me also when I was a young boy and heard my father tell about
the incident. And it has stayed as a positive force in my mind and
life. Where can one find a more positive suggestion than that: "If
God be for us, who can be against us"? It is put in the form of a
question, but it is a positive statement with the power of Almighty
God in back of it.

Just a little over one hundred years ago Abraham Lincoln
lingered with precaution, doubt, and uncertainty, until he finally
said to himself: "I have promised my God that I will do it." He
then, on January 1, 1863, issued his Emancipation Proclamation.
The promises of God to us, and our genuine promise to God are
powerful, positive suggestions.

There is a lot of difference between the man who looks at his
gas gauge and says: "It is half empty," and the man who says: "It
is half full." Likewise, there is a great difference between the one
who finds life half empty, and the man who finds life half full. The
latter is the positive approach.

Most of us do not realize the force that is generated by a vigorous, positive perpetual affirmation of the things for which we are
working and that ought to be. Great things are done under the tug
and pull of an overpowering conviction that God is with us, and
that this is His will. The intensity of our affirmation that something

is God's will is definitely related to the degree of your success or failure. One can be uncertain, or wrong, concerning the will of God. To be sure, however, there is a vast area of life where God reveals Himself clearly. We have not yet really launched out into life with the positive affirmation that we should have.

I once asked a certain man to come to church, to which he replied: "I will start coming to church every Sunday, 'if it be God's will.' " Suddenly he corrected himself by saying, "Come to think of it, going to church is God's will. I will be there." And he was there nearly every Sunday from then. This is an example of what I mean. There are many of these areas where we can be positive, knowing what is the will of God, knowing we can move forward in confidence: "If God be for us, who can be against us?"

The following saying is often attributed to the late Peter Marshall, for he used it so often, but I believe it was Will Rogers who said it originally: "It is not the things in the Bible that I do not understand that bother me, but the things I do understand." There is a vast area of understanding that we have not yet become willing to follow with positive emphasis. That should bother everyone.

A song that was popular when I was a teenager is: "Accentuate the Positive; Eliminate the Negative." I want to discuss how we can do just that when we know so well the will of God and the power that will come from doing it.

I.

Bravely, constantly, and everlastingly affirm, that you will become what God wants you to become. Then say to yourself: "If God be for me in this, who can be against me?" Of course, no one can; you have all the power of heaven with you. No person can have anything greater than that. Do not say: "Sometime I shall try to be what I ought to be." Say instead: "I am a child of God. Right now I am going to be what He wants me to be." Say to yourself: "I know God wants me to go to church," as the man said to whom I referred earlier. Say to yourself: "I know God wants me to be loving, joyful, peaceful; He wants me to have patience, to be kind, to be faithful and gentle, and to exercise self-control." These are some of the things the Scriptures teach in Galatians 5:22, 23. We understand very well that these are the things we should be doing. Say to yourself, positively: "As a child of God, these are the characteristics I will build within myself. It is my birthright to have them."

The habit of positively claiming the promises of God should be a vital reality in our lives. The constant vigorous assertion of: "I am a child of God. I am going to live for Him. I am going to claim His power. I am going to tell the truth. I am going to live by high principles because I am made in the image of God" tends to help bring about these things and the immortal beauty of personality which can be ours.

We can do this if we really want to, but too many of us are like the man who was going to quit smoking. He quit for a while, then he returned to the habit. Someone asked if he didn't have will power. "I have will power," he answered, "but I get tired being bossed around by my will power all the time." Too often that is the problem; we do not want to pay the price of personal discipline. With a positive mind for accomplishment we can do great things.

It will be most helpful if we will affirm positive thoughts, not only silently, but out loud to others. Don't do this in an offensive or obnoxious way. But do it with tact, dignity and esteem. Because of the power of this positive statement a testimony meeting can be so wonderful and effective, when conducted with sincerity and order, particularly when a person shares his newly found life with others.

Noah Webster, the lexicographer, years ago announced that he was going to build a great dictionary, even if it were to take twenty years to do it. That positive affirmation sent him forth to accomplish a great and mammoth task. Twenty-one years later he finally produced a fine two-volume dictionary. Twelve years after that, in 1840, he completed a revision of his original work which contained twelve thousand words and thirty thousand definitions never before published. Likewise, you and I can, by speaking positively to ourselves and others, live and act as God wills for us, not only for a great number of years, but for eternity.

II.

Strongly affirm your ability to be what God wants you to be even against great odds. It will take a lot of faith to have this kind of positive courage. Cicero once said: "A man of courage is also full of faith." This is true when it is true courage. The Scripture, in the New Testament, in the Epistle to the Hebrews, speaking of the courageous of the Old Testament, says that by faith, Enoch, Noah, Abraham, Isaac, Jacob, Joseph and Moses did what they did. The writer of the Epistle to the Hebrews also tells us that: "By faith" writer of the Epistle to the Hebrews also tells us that: "By faith" the Hebrew people passed through the Red Sea, and "by faith" the walls of Jericho came tumbling down. Against great odds, these great people developed faith, courage, and a positive outlook that carried them through.

Some of them were jeered and laughed at. Noah was ridiculed when he built the ark. You will find the same situation when you determine to do what you should do for God, for your family, or even for yourself. However, it is a good thing to remember that you were not designed to be dominated by those who ridicule. Neither were you designed to be dominated by the evils of the world, nor by those who do not know any better than to ridicule and to work against you. You were not designed to be dominated by sin, vice, or evil habit. You were designed by God to rise above the sin of this world—to rise above the negativism that would sap your courage and ability and blunt your moral sensibility.

When the enemy threatens and it appears you may fail, say to yourself, once and for all: "I will have no part of this weakness, this wickedness, this negativism. I do not want it. I will not touch it. I was made to hold up my head and walk erect as a child of God. There is something of the image of God within me, and with the help of God I am perfectly able to conquer, even against great odds. Speaking this way, this positive affirmation of what can be done becomes your prayer. History is full of such evidence of the power of prayer.

A book was published in 1957 called *Triumph Over Odds,* edited by J. Donald Adams. It is an anthology of man's unconquerable spirit. The author traces examples of courage from David and Job in the Old Testament, through the trial and crucifixion of Jesus, through St. Augustine, Beethoven, the four chaplains of World War II, and up to and including someone who died as late as 1956.

Says the author: "Not all battles of this world are fought with guns and bombs, or by men massed in great armies. Some of the greatest have been lonely battles, fought by men or women standing alone. . . . Sometimes the fight was with an enemy they could not see—something without material form—an idea, a weakness within themselves, a physical handicap, like blindness, or an illness to be faced and overcome. These lonely battles, these singlehanded triumphs over odds have given some of the greatest stories in man's history." With the power of the positive suggestion, you can stand with these men and women and become what God wants you to be.

Here is a word of caution. Do not be disappointed if you determine today to put all of these ideas to work and do not immediately see results. Continue your positive prayer in a confident manner, and you will soon conquer your sin, your weakness, your disappointment or whatever it may be. Just remember that the divine power within you is thousands of times stronger than the odds against you. A few years ago someone wrote a book called *God Plus One*. You are that *one*. The whole idea is that you and God always form a majority. If you will cast your vote—your influence—with God, no power can overcome you.

III.

Never allow yourself to be troubled because you are being watched, laughed at or ridiculed.

If Noah had been bothered unduly by those who laughed at him, he would never have completed the ark. If Nehemiah had let those who laughed at him bother him, he would never have rebuilt the walls. I am watched every time I go from my home to the church. I am watched every time I drive into the church parking lot and when I drive out again. I have been laughed at and talked about many times. If I were to let such things bother me, I would just curl up and die. All I can do is accept it and get used to it. A strong, positive, affirmative emphasis will enable a person to rise above laughter and ridicule. Certainly Noah, Nehemiah, and all the great have shown us that one can rise above, rather than be troubled unduly by it.

When the times of laughter and ridicule come, remember, once again, you are a child of God and are not inferior to others who would jeer and tear you apart. You can stand up in the midst of their derision, and walk erect as a child of the King, a complete person, master of the situation.

You will always be tempted to take shortcuts in the game of life. The people who laugh and ridicule will try to get you to just lower your standards a bit. They will tell you that there is an easier way —a way of dishonesty, etc. Many of these people lack ambition. Their lives are negative, with no positive push. They think you can be successful and get by if you just know the right people and pull the right strings.

One fellow said that a person could do anything with "pull." "Oh, yeah," said another. "Did you ever try to get through a door with 'pull' when the sign said: 'Push'?" Make up your mind to do things the right way, according to instructions, and push for the positive, affirmative emphasis in your life, with honesty and integrity, regardless of what others do and say.

Let us seek to make our whole outlook on life cheerful and positive. There is no other way to really serve God and succeed in the business of life. A student took a job selling aluminum ware to earn money for college. The first day, timidly and haltingly he went to his first house in door-to-door sales. He rang the doorbell and when the lady of the house opened the door, he very negatively said: "You don't want to buy any of my aluminum ware, do you?" She replied: "You are right. I don't," and shut the door. He was so defeated that he gave up right then.

Later when he reported to the veteran salesman what had happened, the more experienced man said: "Tomorrow I will work the opposite side of the street, and when you ring the doorbell, I will wave to you as a symbol of the fact that there is one of experience working with you who is ready to help you by giving assurance that you can do it." The next day they went out and with the assurance of the presence of another and the positive assurance in his mind that it could be done, he became successful.

In the business of life, you can know there is a Presence—the Presence of Almighty God—and you can know, that if He be for you, which He is, no one can stand against you. Remember that the positive assurance of *God Plus One* makes a majority. That *one* is you.

PRAYER: Great God of eternal assurance, give me the courage to cast my vote for and with You, that I and others whom I may touch may know we can become what You want us to be. Amen.

4. HOW TO WIN OVER SELF-DOUBT

"I can do all things in him that stengtheneth me"

(Philippians 4:13, ASV).

ONCE WHEN MY FAMILY AND I WERE AT A LAKE, I DECIDED to see if I had courage enough to go up the high slide and then sail down into the deep water. As I approached the climb up the slide, my courage began to fail me; however, I kept going. While going up the steps, I noticed that the name of the slide was "American," and that the name, American, was on each step. I further noticed that the last two syllables of the word were: "I CAN." This became to me a positive suggestion, helping me to say to myself: "I can do it." And I did. Now I have no problem at all doing that sort of thing. I won over self-doubt.

Concerning so many things of life, it is really foolish to say: "I can't." However, it is quite understandable since we are mortal human beings, and we see our apparent microscopic talent and ability. Thus we shrink and become small as we face our "mountain of duty."

We have our bad days and our good days. We rise; we fall. We have a pendulum of emotion within our spirits, "bonging" back and forth from excessive elation to excessive depression. Thus in our low moments of failure, self-doubt starts eating away at us, and if we are not careful, we will be completely obsessed with the spirit of "I can't."

A helpful thing to remember when we are confronted with this problem, is that the problem is a universal one. You do not find that any of the great men of history said that they felt equal to their task. The Apostle Paul was always asking, "Who will be able to do it?" It was only in Christ that he was finally able to say: "I can do all things in Him who strengthens me." God has said that His grace is fulfilled in weakness. Therein lies our hope for winning over self-doubt.

Certainly one of the outstanding examples of self-doubt was in

33

the life of Moses. Even a novelist could hardly invent the dramatic facts and factors that lie at the heart of the life of this man, Moses. He was the son of slaves, condemned to death because he was a boy. He was sheltered in the silence of his home, his little voice quickly hushed every time he started to cry for fear the Egyptian taskmasters would hear him and put him to death. To further hide and protect him, he was put into a little ark and launched to sail on the Nile. His voice was heard by the daughter of the king who had come to bathe. She took him, and, with the help of his mother, she reared Moses, giving him all the advantages of kingly birth.

The day came when Moses found out who he was, and that he was identified with the slaves who lived in Goshen. One day he saw an Egyptian beating one of his brethren. A fire swelled up in Moses and he killed the Egyptian. As a result he had to flee from the country, and for forty years was in the wilderness. After forty years, he saw a burning bush that would not be consumed as it burned. From the bush came the voice of God, telling him to "Go down into Egypt's land and set your people free." Moses, like man today, countered with his three excuses as to why he could not do what was expected of him.

Thus, we find a man overcome by self-doubt, but a man who, with the help of God, was able to overcome his self-doubt.

Let's take a look at his self-doubt in his three excuses, and how he and we overcome them.

I.

We find that Moses' first response was: "Who am I, that I should go unto Pharaoh, and that I should bring forth the children of Israel out of Egypt?" (Exodus 3:11). Is that not often our response when someone comes to us and gives us a job that looks so big we cannot seem to see over it? "Who am I? Why, you should get someone else. I do not have the time, the ability, the intelligence. . . ." And so it goes.

When Moses said: "Who am I?" he probably meant that he was an ordinary man, a son of slaves. St. Augustine, before he became a man of God, was a wild, wild young man. He tells about it in his confessions. He lived for awhile in Carthage, where he studied. While there he went to the place of worship. One day a beautiful girl came in, and he forgot all about worship, watching the girl. He did bow his head for a time. Then she was gone. He came again and again, thinking he might see her. Finally, one day, she did return, and he followed her home and proposed to her.

She replied: "No, I cannot, for I am the daughter of slaves." The lovely lady turned away from the great Augustine because she was shackled by her enslaved heritage and environment.

This is what Moses and we have said to God: "Who am I?" Who are we, and what do we have? We are people, filled with the breath of life, created in the image of God, as children of God, to do great things for Him. That is who we are, and thus the excuse of "Who am I?" will not stand up under any kind of analysis.

II.

The second excuse Moses gave, and so do we, was: "They will not believe me, nor hearken unto my voice. . ." (Exodus 4:1).

We seem to know just how we are going to fail before we ever start. This is the salesman's greatest problem. "How will I get the potential customer to believe me?" It is sometimes a problem, a real problem, in communicating the Good News of God. How will we get the people to believe all these good things we have found to be true? Thus, we are quick to say: "I cannot witness. I cannot tell anyone else about the Lord." Our worst self-doubt is a fear of not being, or appearing, believable.

We find, however, that God told Moses that He could get the people to believe him. God made it clear that He would be with Moses all the way and would reinforce him. I think God reinforced Moses with a spirit of sincerity. If we tell what is truly in our hearts, we will become more believable. It is that which is unbelievable that people will not believe, and we make it unbelievable by not believing it ourselves.

We cannot share what we do not have. However, if we share what we truly believe, people will listen. People do not want to hear our doubts. What people want to hear is what we really believe with all our hearts. Whenever a person says to me: "I believe," and then proceeds to say what it is he believes, I will listen. I have heard many people, even those who do not agree with Billy Graham, say of him: "I love to hear him speak, because I know he believes what he is saying and is deeply convinced in his own heart that it is true."

Let us believe in our cause, and people will listen to our voices and many will believe. As long as we believe in what we are saying, this second excuse will not stand as valid.

III.

The third excuse that Moses makes as he is called to his particular task is: "I am not eloquent."

"Oh, my Lord, I am not eloquent" (Exodus 4:10). That is an

excuse that nearly every teacher, minister, lawyer, actor or public speaker of any kind has made at some time.

I find that many people who do not speak before a group, such as addressing a class, a club gathering, a rally, or a church congregation, will look at a person who does, and say: "It is very easy for him, for all he has to do is mount the platform, and his mouth automatically comes open and the words just purr out." I heard a lady recently say that about a singer: "All he has to do is open his mouth and the music just flows out."

Now, if it were true that certain people just naturally do certain things requiring much skill, the excuse of Moses might hold up to a certain degree. It is true that some people have leanings in the direction of skills and ability in specific areas, but if you will study the background and the lives of people who are capable and skilled in speaking, writing, singing, acting, law, organization, building, farming, or whatever it may be, you will find that they spent many lonely and tedious hours learning how to do it. They spent much time practicing, with all the discouragements and embarrassing moments that this brings. No man is born with all the skills and eloquence that we think comes so naturally in other people. Every person has a certain amount of self-doubt, but one of the ways to overcome it is to set a goal and work at self-development.

Moses then went on to say: "Not only am I not eloquent, but I am slow of speech." He may have meant that he stuttered. Yet we find in history that some of the greatest speakers were men who had overcome stuttering. The point I make here is that the power of your life does not depend on it being easy for you to do certain things. The power of your life and your ability to overcome self-doubt depends upon the degree to which you have a dynamic passionate faith and the extent to which you are willing to go in working and praying to develop your abilities.

A young Chinese once asked for a history of Christians, not a history of Christianity. He wanted to know, he said, when Christians had first stopped following Christ, but had continued to call themselves Christians. He took Christ seriously, but he believed most Christians were falling far short of the name of Christ, too filled with self-doubt, negativism, not taking seriously the life and teachings of the Master.

Think of those first men around the Saviour. They were not men who were natural and eloquent at the task to which the Master called them. They were fishermen, tax-collectors—rather offensive in many ways. Yet Peter preached on Pentecost in such a way that three thousand, by the power of the Holy Spirit, came to know the salvation of the Lord. These men were men who had come to possess an inflamed faith, and had learned to stick to truth and tell it with all the vitality of their beings. They were men who had overcome self-doubt.

God finally told Moses that He would send his brother along to speak for him. I am sure that God knew all along that once Moses got started and got the feel of doing a job he would want to do his own speaking, as he did after he overcame his self-doubt. We find his speeches in Deuteronomy, with their precision of structure, their detail and eloquent imagery. Moses tells about the serpent crawling over the rocks at high noon. He describes the eagle swooping down, and the eaglets fluttering and landing on the big eagle's wings. He vividly tells about the scorpion and the cloudless sky. He effectively deals with visibilities, doing the very thing he had previously said he could not do. With his self-doubt out of the way, vast throngs of Israelites cling to his words. This man knew what he was talking about.

When I graduated from high school, I was fighting what God wanted me to do. In fact, I announced to myself that never again would I ever have to stand before a group, large or small, and say anything. The class plays and the book reports were behind me, and never again would I stand and address a group in any way. I was completely obsessed with self-doubt. Three years later, with at least a certain degree of confidence, I started my seven years of study for the ministry.

This same God who helped Moses overcome his self-doubt, and who helped me overcome my defeatist attitude, will help you overcome your self-doubt if you are willing to follow Him and obey His commands. If God says: "Go down into Egypt"—go. If God asks you to speak for Him—speak for Him. If God asks you to sing for Him—sing for Him. If God asks you to work for the good of your community and church, and to spread some cheer where it is needed—do it and do it soon.

When a person develops a humble and reasonable confidence, he then possesses one of the greatest gifts that God has bestowed upon us. Without this, people become pessimistic and a negative influence in this world. A pessimist is a man who wears both suspenders and a belt, has no confidence in either, and carries a safety pin. The spirit of optimism is the spirit that makes the tea-kettle sing even when up to its neck in hot water. Overcome self-doubt. Become optimistic and sing.

Dr. Norman Vincent Peale tells about a man who approached him with a peculiar intensity of manner, and asked: "May I talk to you about a matter of desperate importance to me?" The man went on: "I have a terrible disbelief in myself. I have no confidence. I am very discouraged and depressed. In fact," he lamented, "I'm just about sunk. Here I am, forty years old. Why is it that all my life I have been tormented by inferiority feelings, by lack of confidence, by self-doubt?"

After discussing the problem kindly with the man, Dr. Peale wrote out this verse and gave it to him: "I can do all things through Christ which strengtheneth me" (Philippians 4:13). The man pulled himself up, stood quietly for a moment and then squared his shoulders and walked into the night. Later, the man reported that it seemed incredible that a few words from the Bible could do so much for a person.

It does not happen to everyone in the same way, but you, too, can overcome self-doubt by becoming truly aware that you are a child of God, that you must sincerely believe in Him and respond to what He wants you to do, knowing that in Him you, like Moses, can do it.

PRAYER: Almighty and gracious God, help me to find Thy way and walk in it in all confidence and trust in the truth. Amen.

5. WALK ON THE SUNNY SIDE OF THE STREET

". . . . but be of good cheer, I have overcome the world"
                                                    (John 16:33).

WHEN I WAS A TEENAGER, SOMEONE GAVE ME A BOOK FOR boys to read. Among other suggestions that would be helpful to a young man's health, was the suggestion that he walk on the sunny side of the street so that he might benefit from the health-giving rays of the sun. I do not know just how much more vitamin D one gets by walking a block in the sun than he would get walking in the shade, but it certainly gives an aura of cheer to experience a nice pleasant sunny day, especially after a few stormy, cloudy ones.

I understand that on a famous sundial was written: "I record none but hours of sunshine." Now would it not be a wonderful thing if each of us would make that a life goal, to record, to remember, and to share with others warm-hearted cheerfulness? That would be walking on the sunny side of the street of life.

Look Magazine, describing a young couple in Southern California, worded it this way: "They have two daughters, two cars, three bedrooms, one cat, a few books, a few records, and a couple of the most unwaveringly sunny dispositions in all of sunny California."[1] A good cheerful pleasant disposition has always been likened to bright warm sunshine. On the pathway of life walk on the sunny side of the street.

In the sixteenth chapter of John, Jesus speaks plainly to the disciples about what is to come. He will be crucified. He will go away. The disciples will be scattered. They shall have trial and tribulation. But in the midst of it all, He tells them to be of good cheer because He has overcome the world. He is telling them to walk on the sunny side of the street. "Be of good cheer."

It is a fact that life is going to present every one of us with both the sweet and the bitter, and it is most unfortunate that many

[1]*Look,* September 25, 1962, page 34.

people seem unable to remember the pleasant, agreeable things. Some people, when you meet them, always have a depressing story to tell of how life is treating them. They tell you about accidents, narrow escapes, hurts, slights and afflictions that they have suffered. The bright days and sunny cheerful experiences are seldom mentioned. They recall only the disagreeable, the ugly, the depressing. The cloudy days make such an impression upon them that they seem to think it is cloudy all the time. One fellow said that was the kind of a person from whom he would like to borrow money, because with such a dark and dismal outlook toward life, the person would never expect to get it back.

On the other hand there are those who are just the opposite. One of my seminary professors was a close friend of Dr. Sam Shoemaker, and he often told us of how every time he saw Dr. Shoemaker, the man had some wonderful, pleasant experience to tell him about. He walked on the sunny side of the street of life. Those who do, talk of pleasant things, good times, and inspiring experiences. We all know people, I am sure, who have had many kinds of misfortunes, problems, losses, heartaches, and yet who seldom speak of them. In the midst of all, they find good things and talk about them. These are the people who attract us and inspire us. These are the people we love.

The habit of walking on the sunny side of the street of life is a result of holding kind, loving, cheerful thoughts in the mind, while the gloomy, dark and dismal character is formed by letting one's thoughts dwell upon the negative, the harsh, and the unkind, until the mind becomes set, as though cemented in darkness, and the life radiates only gloom. You do not want to be a gloomy kind of person.

We discuss now, in some detail, what the mind often does, what it should do, and how it can do it, leading us to the sunny side of the street of life.

I.

Some people's minds are like a junk shop. They contain much of great value but are mixed in with a great deal of rubbish. This is not all bad. Such a person is not completely evil. He has no system or order. His mind simply retains everything—good, bad, or indifferent. These would be what Dr. James Whitcomb Brougher, calls "lopsided people." He tells about a man who was becoming deaf. The doctor told him he would have to quit cluttering up his mind with liquor. He did, and, just as so often happens when we free the mind and body of what ought not to be there, he got better.

He grew to hear very well again. Then, after a while, he resumed his drinking, and became more deaf than before. The doctor asked him why he had done it. He replied: "I soon discovered that things I heard, I didn't like as well as the things I drank." I am afraid he was letting his life become cluttered like a junk shop.

Some people get into the habit of doing certain things and thinking certain thoughts, and don't want to throw them out. Thus mental storehouses and lives become clogged with all sorts of rubbish. If we are going to get over to the sunny side of the street, we will have to get rid of the mental rubbish that keeps a dark cloud hovering over our life. Get rid of the burden of non-essential, meaningless things. Every day we see people handicapped because they never want to let go of anything; thus the attic, the garage, and every corner are filled with rubbish.

The practice of throwing away rubbish of all kinds is necessary. It is the only way to let the sunshine come in. No life can walk in the sunshine when clouded with evil, unhappy, resentful, retaliating vicious thoughts. The mental sky must be clear or there can be no efficiency, no enthusiasm, clearness, or brightness in life. The mind must not be like a junk shop with a strange mixture of disorderly things.

II.

The great hope and good news is that the mind can be filled with truth, beauty and sunshine.

When Jesus said, in the midst of all that was to happen, "Be of good cheer," He was essentially saying that all dark and dismal things can be put away, overcome, and that cheerful thoughts can rule. The Apostle Paul said: ". . . but one thing I do, forgetting what lies behind and straining forward to what lies ahead. . ." (Philippians 3:13, rsv). Paul knew how to throw out the old and dark and take on the bright and the new. The Apostle Paul's conversion was a moving from the dark side to the sunny side of the street of life where God has intended that man should walk. Man was first made to walk on the sunny side in the Garden of Eden, but man soon chose to walk on the dark side much of the time.

When man gets a real vision of what God had made him for—in the image of God—he becomes ashamed for harboring unworthy, disagreeable, depressing thoughts, as ashamed as he would be if he had stolen something. Man was simply not designed to express discord, but rather was expected to express harmony, love, truth, beauty and happiness. Man was not made to walk in the shadow of life, for he becomes anemic, colorless. He was made to walk in the sunshine of life and to obtain the golden glow of personality.

You can start now walking on the sunny side. If you have unkind thoughts, hard feelings toward others, if you are trying to get even with someone who has hurt you, or if you are suffering from jealousy, envy, or hatred, you are walking in the shadows. Decide now to kill these dark, damaging emotions, and get out of the darkness into the light. Think of Christ and the spirit He showed when put on the cross, and say to yourself: "I have not been as manly, as friendly, as considerate, and as forgiving as I should have been." This spirit of confession and asking for forgiveness with a desire to start anew will get you out of the shadows and into the sunshine.

A story was told to me by someone who was riding with Bishop Showers one day when the Bishop drove his big Buick onto a very narrow bridge. At the center of the bridge they met a big, burly man in a truck, and they could not pass on the narrow bridge. The man shouted from his truck window: "I never back up from any fool." Bishop Showers, as he was putting his car in reverse, answered: "I always do." They said that they had never seen a man back a truck off a bridge as fast as that truck driver did. Bishop Showers walked on the sunny side of life. Remember, it can be done.

III.

It is good to remember, also, that the person who walks on the sunny side, radiates good cheer and happiness to everyone, and sees and brings out good things in others.

There is something good to be found in just about everyone. The better person we are, the more sunny our personality, and the more we will see the good in others. I heard about a woman who always said something good about everyone. You could mention the most disliked person in the community, and she would find something good to say about that person. I think it is wonderful to be that way. One day someone said: "Let us talk about the devil and see if she comes up with something good to say about him." They talked about the devil for a few minutes. Finally this woman spoke up and said: "Well, you certainly have to give him credit for being persistent."

As you walk the sunny side of life, learn to put a tolerant interpretation upon other people's motives. They probably did not intend to slight or injure you. Show your charitable sunny side to everyone, and you will be surprised at the effect of your attitude upon yourself and those with whom you come in contact. In fact, the kind, cheerful, sympathetic thought shown toward your enemies will work toward their conversion and work like a leaven in their characteristics, helping to change them for the better much quicker than revenge and trying "to get even" would do.

If someone should say a mountain of unkind things about you and only a pebble of good, forget the mountain, but remember the pebble. That is the way God is toward us. He says that He will not remember our sins against us any more because of Christ's sacrificial and atoning death on the cross for us. If we will practice the art of forgetting the mountains of evil, we will learn to love and see good where we once hated, to admire where we once despised, to praise where we once criticized, and to help where we once hindered.

A friend of mine had a neighbor who became angry with him and would not speak. They met often, but still the neighbor remained silent. One day they went around the same corner rapidly and met head on. The neighbor cursed and became angry. My friend said, with a smile: "Well, my good neighbor, you can talk, can't you?" The man then chuckled and replied: "All right, you old fool, you win." They were on good speaking terms from then on, because my friend, who walked on the sunny side of life, saw some good in this angry neighbor.

President Lincoln had the qualities which we have been discussing. He appointed Edwin Stanton to his cabinet, though Stanton had criticized Lincoln harshly and unfairly. The great Lincoln brushed aside all this and appointed him because he thought Stanton to be suited for the job. It was a surprise to the nation, and a friend asked Lincoln if he thought he could control Stanton. Lincoln replied with a story about a Methodist minister whom he knew. Speaking of the minister, Lincoln said: "When he got wrought up in a high pitch of excitement in his prayers or exhortations, they put bricks into his pockets to hold him down. We may have to treat Stanton that way, but I'm going to let him jump awhile first."

It is reported that soon after Stanton's appointment, a committee of senators met with the president and urged him to make a clean sweep. They wanted him to appoint six other new members to the cabinet, in addition to Stanton. Lincoln listened with courtesy and patience. Then, with a twinkle in his eyes, he said: "Gentlemen, your request for a change of the whole cabinet, because I have made one change, reminds me of the farmer who was much troubled by skunks. They annoyed his household at night and his wife insisted that he get rid of them. One moonlight night he loaded his shotgun and stationed himself in the yard to watch for the intruders. After some time, his wife, in the house, heard the shotgun go off. When the farmer came in, she asked him: "What luck

I killed only one. He raised such a fearful stink that I concluded that it was best to let the other six go." The senators had a cheerful laugh, and nothing more was said about changes in the cabinet.

Remember, Jesus said, "Be of good cheer." Combine the spirit of forgiveness and good will with a sense of humor, and you will find that you — like Jesus, like the disciples, like the Apostle Paul, and like Lincoln — can walk on the sunny side of life.

PRAYER: Gracious God, thou who hast created us for happiness, give us the spirit of good cheer, and the courage to share it with others as witness of what life can mean when lived in the golden glow of Christ our Saviour. Amen.

6. HOW TO MASTER OUR BAD MOODS

"Go forth, and stand upon the mount before the Lord"
(I Kings 19:11).

AN ARTICLE IN THE MAGAZINE, *Our Home*, OCTOBER, 1962, is entitled, "Enjoy Each Shining Hour." Now is that not a wonderful thing to do? However, not everyone is enjoying each shining hour of each day. We seem to have too many evil days with our bad moods.

There are days when things seem to be difficult; everything seems to go wrong. Such days bring on bad moods of depression. They cause us to be moody, resentful, and of bad disposition. However, such a time is just the opportunity to show that of which you are made. It may be difficult, but it is just the time to show that you can rise above the situation and not give in to moodiness or depression.

I heard about a man who was having a bad day at home, and said to his wife: "I'm going to find out who is boss in this house."

She quickly replied: "You will be happier if you don't."

(He really had a bad day then, but he had asked for it.)

Of course, it is comforting to know that the problem of depression and bad moods has existed since time began. Even the great people of all ages have had to cope with it. The Prophet Elijah found himself depressed. He had had a long and difficult battle with King Ahab and Queen Jezebel. It appeared to him that everyone was on the side of the pagan worship of Baal, and that no one was for God. As a result, he went and hid himself in a lonely cave.

As the depressed Elijah sat there in that dismal cave, the Lord asked him what he was doing. He replied that everyone was for Baal, that he was the only one left serving God, and that they were trying to kill him. Then, that lifting and inspiring voice of hope, the voice of God spoke to him: "Go forth, and stand upon the mount before the Lord." The Lord assured Elijah that there were still seven thousand who had not bowed to Baal but were serving the Lord. In our moods of depression and anger, we often imagine things to be about seven thousand times worse than they are.

When you get up in the morning, blue, discouraged, moody and disagreeable, make up your mind to pray to God that, come what may, you are going to make this a "red-letter day" and not a day in which your spirits are "in the red." Someone has said: "When it is hardest to pray, you most need to pray." Indeed, it is difficult to pray when in a bad mood, but it is a time when we certainly ought to pray.

Man seems to be a rather lazy being. When things are difficult for him, the temptation to avoid facing a difficult situation and conquering it is great. Likewise, the temptation to give way to a moody, hateful, temperamental disposition is also great. According to one person: "Temperamental means 95 per cent temper and 5 per cent mental."

How can we handle our bad moods?

I.

First of all, we must determine that we are going to, in some way, grab the demons of temperament and moodiness and throw them out of our lives.

Such things as anger, irritation, sour feelings, depression, and moody thoughts are psychological devils and need to be conquered. They not only disturb the mind, but injure the body by developing poisons and foul acids that eat away at our cells. They prevent proper circulation and hamper proper breathing. They wear upon and tear away nervous tissue. They drive away hopefulness, destroy high motives, and lower mental efficiency. Just as Jesus drove the demons out of those who were infested and shackled by alien spirits, so, likewise, they must be driven from our lives.

If you are moody, irritable or despondent, and find that it is hindering your development and success, you will never conquer it by brooding. To nurse such feelings along only aggravates them.

Certainly Elijah had to rid himself of his moody disposition. Understandable as it is that he should feel the way he did after seeing the vicious Jezebel, Elijah could not afford to let the demon of depression overcome him. God had work for him to do, and so He told him to "Go forth, and stand upon the mount before the Lord."

We, too, need to get out of the valley of depression and "stand upon the mount before the Lord." When we do, we will find that, in the presence of God, things are about seven thousand times better than we thought they were.

II.

The cure for bad moods is not complete by just throwing them out; we need to take on good moods to fill the place the bad ones once occupied.

In spite of our many jokes about there being nothing between the ears and about a doctor looking into one ear and out the other, the mind must be filled with something. I recently heard a definition of an "aching void" — a headache.

It will require some effort of will to "stand upon the mount of the Lord," where we are inspired to rise above bad moods and depression. In the presence of the living God, however, we can hold positive thoughts, the opposite from those thoughts which depress. Thus the mood will be positively reversed from depression to a certain degree of genuine elation. This is the way God intended that we should live.

When you are the victim of ugly moods pray to God for good moods, and say to yourself: "This is not the way God wants me to live. This is not the way for me to be my best self, for the Creator never intended that I should be dominated with lower moods."

The psalmist felt the need for higher thoughts, "The Lord is the strength of my life. . . . in this will I be confident" (Psalm 27:1,3).

Know that you can "stand upon the mount before the Lord," that He is your strength. With confidence in Him, recall the most delightful experience you have ever had, your happiest days, knowing that you can have them again. Hold constantly in your mind the things you have enjoyed and the promise that you shall have them again. Reach out for the positive, joyous thought when bad moods threaten. Call upon God to give you hope, and in your mind picture the bright and wonderful life God has intended for you. Where there is no hope, faith itself will be dead.

Two men were fishing, and one said to the other: "Hope is a wonderful thing."

"Indeed," said the other. "One little nibble keeps you fishing all day."

"Yes," said his companion, "hope will keep the fisherman patiently waiting for a bite, but when he gets home, if he has to wait ten minutes for a bite to eat, he is irritated."

We have to keep up our patience and hope at home also.

At home, at work, at school, and in church, or wherever you are, seek to fill yourself with happy spirited thoughts, and you will be surprised to see how quickly the demons of blackness and gloom will be crowded out. They cannot bear the light of joy, gladness, high morale and good moods. No, we cannot just get rid of the bad mood and remain neutral. We must replace it with the positive good mood.

III.

Finally, it is good to note that until we can get rid of bad moods, we can never be a success at the business of life.

No man who is at the mercy of his bad moods is a free person. You can be a slave to bad moods just as you can be a slave to liquor, tobacco, or "to any taint or vice whose corruption inhabits our frail blood" (Shakespeare).

When I was in grade school, I was moody and had a vicious temper. The other boys knew it and would throw snowballs at me just to see me smolder with anger and then explode. One day I made some very hard snowballs and fortified myself around the corner of the school. When some of the boys came by, I began to pelt them right in their faces with one after another of these rock-hard snowballs. I got into some real trouble because of the incident. Then I made up my mind to be cheerful, to cease my moodiness, and to control my temper. I did change, and had friends. Already the business of life as a boy in grade school was much more successful.

If a person must check up on his moods each morning to see whether he is fit to go ahead with a project, if he must continuously gauge his activities according to whether his morale is up or down, he is a slave and cannot be successful or happy.

How different is the person who can rise in the morning, cheerful and happy, confident that he can meet the rigors of the day with at least a reasonable degree of healthy mood and expression. This man will do his best work. He will get along with people. People will like to meet him and work with him. Outward circumstances will not hinder him to any great degree, because he has the good mood so essential for life.

God helped Elijah overcome bad moods because He had work for him to do. God will help you overcome any bad mood with which you are threatened. He will give you a good spirit. He will answer the psalmist's prayer: "Create in me a clean heart, O God; and renew a right spirit within me" (Psalm 51:10).

When we go forth and "stand upon the mount before the Lord," holding ourselves steadfastly to the task no matter how hard or disagreeable it may be, with prayer and communion with Him, we will soon be able to learn and develop the right spirit, the good mood, that will enable us to live the good life.

PRAYER: O Lord, when my life is beclouded by the threatening storms of depression and ugly moods, help me to drive them away and renew a right spirit within me. Amen.

7. WHY DON'T PEOPLE LIKE ME?

*"And Jesus increased in wisdom and in stature, and in favour with
God and man"*   *(Luke 2:52).*

"WHY DON'T PEOPLE LIKE ME?" THIS HAS BEEN ASKED MANY
times in different ways. "Why can't I impress people?" "Why do I
always seem to do the wrong thing and say the wrong thing?"

Surely the desire to impress people and be liked cannot be completely bad.

Indeed, we are told that one of the most important tasks we can
undertake is to develop our ability to get along with other people.
It has been said that 50 per cent of doing a job well is getting along
with other people. Yet lately, more detailed research has found that
85 per cent of a person's ability to stay on the job successfully
depends upon his ability to get along with people. You can be a
real whiz on the job and still get fired if you cannot get along with
people. On the other hand you can do a poorer job and remain on
the payroll if you can just get along well with other people.

It is important to ourselves to get along with people and to have
people like us. We want to be liked. Yet, we are told to beware
when all speak well of us. A too easy popularity means a too easy
and too flexible personality. One pastor said he always felt his
sermon was a failure if it did not make someone mad. There is an
element of truth to this side of the picture, but being disliked does
not necessarily indicate virtue. The criminal, Al Capone, was hated,
but that did not make him good.

It is quite possible to be charming and liked and yet be a bad
person. Also, it is quite possible to be unappreciated and be a good
person. There is no set formula. But the problem for many who are
reasonably good people is: "Why don't people like me?"

I.

Maybe people do like us and we just don't think they do.

I read the other day about a little girl making faces at a bulldog.
Her mother scolded her and asked her to stop it. "Well, he started

it," said the little girl. That would not be hard to believe for it isn't difficult for a bulldog to look ugly. But you know this is the bulldog's natural look and the girl only *thought* the dog was deliberately making faces at her. Actually the dog was innocent.

In similar ways, we sometimes think people don't like us when they actually do. Perhaps they don't like to do the same things we do, maybe they don't always agree with us, maybe they don't go to the same places we go, maybe we don't think they look at us just right, maybe we think they are talking about us, and so we conclude that they don't like us.

We react in various ways when we feel people don't like us. Sometimes we just pull into our shell, like a hermit. Sometimes we fight—make faces back, like the little girl. But this behavior is costly. People who live with the idea that they must return every ugly face they think they see, every ugly act that they think is directed toward them or every dislike that they think is hurled their way, will have a never-ending, profitless job. They will go through life just making faces. They harm themselves far more than they harm others. Not every ugly look, not every slight, not every evil toward us means that we are not liked.

II.

However, let us admit that there are people who do not like us.

Some people do not like you. Some people do not like me. Why? One reason is that preferences differ. Some people just do not respond to the kind of person we are. A perfectly pleasant man walked down the street in Chicago one day and met a drunk, who said, "I don't like you! Wipe that smile off your face!" Well, you cannot argue with a person's taste. You like grapefruit, or you do not. A person responds to your kind of smile, or he does not. Then, too, some people are nearly impossible to please. They criticize others because they dislike themselves. In their rage against themselves, they try to take it out on you.

Speaking of people you cannot please, people who do not like anyone, Dr. Otto Gruber says that they have cultivated meanness to the point that when they die, they even resist embalming. It is a waste of time to try to get certain people to like us. They do not need us; they need Christ. Be more concerned about their knowing Christ than about their liking you.

Another reason why some people do not like you is that, at times, your Christian ideals cause you to stand alone. This sometimes makes enemies. Christ said it would happen. It is like Edna St. Vincent Millay's saying: "If you refuse to be a regimented mouse, you will not be liked by the cats." To some, you are simply a square.

Yet, when the chips are down, some of these people who do not like you will come to you for help and guidance because they know you have something strong and stable that they do not have.

III.

Since we cannot get everybody to like us, what should we do and how should we live?

The first thing we should do is to concentrate less on pleasing people and more on pleasing God. Right here is where our text comes in. "And Jesus increased in wisdom and in stature, and in favour with God and man." Jesus, growing in favor with man did not mean that everybody liked Him. They did not. There were those who, for their own perverted reasons, hated Him to death. But, we read in Mark 12:37: "The common people heard him gladly," for He made all life seem brighter for all who came to Him. First, He grew in favor with God. Seek first to please God. Learn to please God by learning to do His will through prayer, public worship and Christian service in church and community. Just be a real Christian, pleasing God.

At a luncheon meeting the other day, a man said to me: "I believe that a Christian should be a radically different person." Now, he is right. But be careful not to push your Christian idealism into fanaticism. Do not boast of how different you are. That is not the way to grow in favor with either God or man. There are so many areas of life where it is pleasing to God to acknowledge that we are like others. At the communion table, at the altar, beneath the cross, we all become very much alike—in humility, sinners saved by grace.

Another thing we should do is to try to understand people and see them as a part of their heredity, environment, decision, education and experience. That is what has made them, and has made you. Says Robert Frost: "The shortest way out is through." Think of what some people have been through. Perhaps you would be as stubborn, as indifferent, as ugly, as holier-than-thou, if you had come by the same road.

Then, we should try to love people. It may seem hard but it is not impossible. In fact, love is the central message of Christianity. We love because He first loved us. This is the key to the Christian life. There are, not far from you, people who need your love. There are sick people, lonely people, confused people, repulsive people, angry people, moody people, cynical and sad people. They need our love. They need the outreach of our helping hand and need to know the magic of the word, friend.

Do not overlook the cultivation of your sense of humor. Lincoln never lost his sense of humor. Once when speaking of a man for whom he had little admiration, he said: "He doesn't even have the brains of a donkey." The man demanded a public apology, so Lincoln announced: "I am sorry. I take it all back. . . . He does have the brains of a donkey." In one of the Lincoln-Douglas debates, Douglas tried to depreciate Lincoln by announcing to the crowds that Lincoln had at one time been a bartender. When Lincoln rose to speak again, he replied: "The difference between Douglas and me is that while I was behind the bar, Douglas was in front of it." The person who laughs is seldom lonely.

Be sure to listen to people. It may not do you any good, but it surely will them. We never listen enough. Just listen. People want to be heard. In listening, you will perhaps learn why they seem so peculiar to you and vice versa.

Why don't you like me? Come right down to it, that is not really the most important question. Yes, we want to grow in favor with God and man. The God who made you made you to be an individual, to look through your own eyes, with Christ stamped upon the retina, that you might see all things through Him. You are to live through your own spirit motivated by the Holy Spirit to receive for yourself His message of salvation and redemption.

Paul wrote: "Remember that Jesus Christ was raised from the dead, according to my gospel." Notice that He said, "my gospel." He had digested it. It had become a part of him. It gave him faith in the resurrection of the dead. But this made him a strange figure to the Athenians on Mars Hill, because they, steeped in the Greek philosophy, denied the resurrection of the dead.

Like Paul, when our lives are hidden with Christ in God, we do not have to cringe before others and what they think of us, or become militant nothings, or meet the world lying down. Neither do we have to build ourselves up by tearing down others, or make a noise to get attention. When we walk into a room, we should bring a Presence with us, the Presence of Christ.

Living in Christ develops a worthy workman in the sight of God and in favor with man, a kind of confidence of the highest order. When we live in Him, we have the humble right to have that faith in ourselves which brings us self-respect and a sense of worth and dignity, but we are here for something more important than popular acclaim.

Just remember that God made people, Jesus Christ died for people, and that you have been called to understand and serve people.

PRAYER: Give to me the spirit to love more than the desire to be loved, and a desire to serve more than to be served. Amen.

8. LIFE'S BEST ROAD

"This one thing I do, forgetting those things which are behind, and reaching forth unto those things which are before"

(Philippians 3:13).

WHEN A PERSON PLANS FOR A VACATION OR BUSINESS TRIP, he is always interested in finding the best road. The best road is not necessarily the easiest. It depends upon what you want and are looking for. Sometimes, when a person goes on a business trip and time is important, he will probably want the easiest road, for it will, in all probability, get him there and back in less time. Sometimes, when the automobile club or oil company plans your trip for you, you are asked if you want the fastest or most scenic route. If you are driving a test car, chances are that you will want the most challenging road.

One never knows just what he will meet on any of these roads. There are often disappointments, sometimes accidents, and even costly time-consuming delays. One time I took my mother and sister to Colorado, and a road, which I had thought would be blacktop, was heavy gravel, so loose I could hardly keep my 1936 Ford on the grade. That caused an hour's delay. Another time, though I was then only three and one-half years old, I vividly recall an accident and the delay in the doctor's office.

Occasionally, on the road of life, we meet misfortunes, disappointments and what appear to be costly delays. Sometimes, as we travel the road of life, we seek the easy road, but if we do that, we will usually be disappointed. Sometimes we seek the most scenic road, the most exciting, the most glamorous. If this is all we seek, again we are likely to be disappointed.

Sometimes those with stalwart spirit and dignity seek the challenging road. This is certainly honorable and to be commended. Disappointment, discouragement and delays will seldom defeat such a person for he understands life and is able to stand up to it. Usually, he is the kind of person we like to meet, to be with, and to

53

travel with. Of all of those we have mentioned, this person has chosen life's best road. The Apostle Paul has given us in Philippians 3:13, a beautiful and practical outline of how to travel life's best road.

Let us take this verse and break it down into three parts, three clues for traveling life's best road, and discuss them in some detail.

I.

As we travel life's best road, we must specialize in concentration. "This one thing I do," says the Apostle. People who have made a real contribution to life have been people of concentration.

There must be concentration of prayer. If prayer is to be meaningful, it cannot be taken lightly; it cannot be engaged in careless fashion. Prayer is rarely meaningful if we fail to dedicate ourselves to the concentrated practice of prayer. "This one thing I do." I pray.

There must be concentration in study. One cannot today travel life's best road if he does not read and study. Life will simply pass him by. Most people read a daily paper, several magazines, and a few books. In addition to this, the Christian who seeks to travel life's best road, will concentrate in the study of the Bible to find meaning and purpose in his other reading. Concentration in Bible study will influence the Christian's total reading, causing him to select better reading material. There are two ways for us to travel: the broad way that leads to destruction and the narrow way that leads to life. "This one thing I do." I study to know the way, the road that my Lord has outlined for me.

Also, there must be concentration of thought. We must think over what we read, and those things which we make a subject of prayer. A person ought to think before he speaks. He ought to think before he speaks to God. He ought to think about God and God's will for his life. When we read the Bible, we ought to think seriously about what it means to us and the way in which we live.

A person should concentrate in thought as he prepares to witness to others. Someone has said that "The difference between some people and a mirror is that a mirror reflects without speaking, and the people speak without reflecting." Think before you speak. What you can say to one person, you cannot say to another. "This one thing I do." I think.

There must also be concentration of action. People of success, accomplishment and helpfulness in the world have been people who have concentrated all their energy on the doing of things. The Christian concentrates on doing the will of God, after he has thought through and prayed.

The Lord's faithful will always want to concentrate on acting and living as Christians. A man may be a husband, a father, a workman, a Democrat or a Republican, and a Rotarian, but if he is to really live the good life, he will, in all of these areas of life, concentrate on being Christ's man of action. "This one thing I do." In all of life I concentrate on action for God. "This one thing I do." I specialize in concentration for Him.

II.

If we are to travel life's best road, we must specialize in cancellation. "Forgetting those things which are behind." This deals with forgiveness.

It is a strange thing, is it not, that man can launch gleaming rockets and missiles into orbit with considerable success, but is unable to launch himself free from his horrible past. In spite of his conquest of space, he cannot really get his soul off the spiritual launching pad and into the orbit of God. With all of his many spectacular conquests over the material world, man still, all too often, carries within his soul, an ache he cannot quite describe.

Man wants forgiveness for his past sins, but he does not seem to know quite how to make it a reality. Man usually believes that God is beaming pardon toward him, but like an ailing television set, he cannot seem to bring the picture into focus.

One reason we have difficulty getting the picture of forgiveness into focus is that we want to keep on doing too many of the things for which we need to be forgiven. We continue to take moral curves on two wheels, and this is dangerous. Many who are caught in this vicious pattern of living do not like it. In fact, they despise it and want a different life. They want to be clean, but somehow hesitate to do what is required. What can we do?

We can follow the advice of the Apostle Paul: ". . . forgetting those things which are behind . . ." then come clean. We know God will forgive us, but we must change our ways and forgive ourselves.

When a son goes wrong, a good father's heart is broken. The father then, if he possibly can, takes steps to repair the wrong. If the son has stolen, he pays the debt. Should the son be in a hospital, near death from an accident, the father gives blood for a transfusion. If the son is in prison, the father intercedes with the law. He says: "It was wrong, but you have had a change of heart. You are ready to come clean. So, come on, son, let us work it out together."

That is exactly what our Heavenly Father is saying to each of us.

"Come now, and let us reason together, saith the Lord: though your sins be as scarlet, they shall be as white as snow; though they be red like crimson, they shall be as wool" (Isaiah 1:18). That He might make this invitation very clear, God has placed at the center of history a cross with His Son on it. This cross has become sort of a continental divide of time, a scarlet cross for the scarlet sin of man.

In John, Christ said: "If I be lifted up from the earth, I will draw all men unto me." That cross is there to lift up that which has been let down, to bring forgiveness where there is guiltiness. From that cross, Christ speaks to all time, and says that your sin is forgiven. ". . . if we walk in the light, as he is in the light, we have fellowship with one another, and the blood of Jesus his son cleanses us from all sin" (I John 1:7, RSV). The person who is ready to come clean, "forgetting those things which are behind," will find forgiveness and will find in Christ his life, and the life is the light of men.

When God forgives, He forgets. The Scriptures state that He will not remember our sins against us. To follow life's best road, we must specialize in forgiving ourselves and "forgetting those things which are behind."

III.

In traveling life's best road we must specialize in anticipation. ". . . reaching forth unto those things which are before." You cannot really travel life's best road as a Christian without enthusiastic anticipation of greater things to come. When joyful anticipation dies, carelessness sets in, and when carelessness enters, one tends toward the lesser road and a drifting away from the center of spiritual truth. Do not travel the road of life looking for trouble, faults, failures, the ugly and the deformed. Do not look for and anticipate the distorted road. Anticipate and find the road God made for you. Learn, with the Apostle Paul, to anticipate the well-lighted straight and narrow road. Hold to those things that give joy, that are helpful and inspiring, and you will transform your whole way of looking at things. You will then be eager to reach forward to greater things.

Part of the Christian's joyful anticipation is the realization that he has not finished anything and will not in this life. His great anticipation is the life to come. When I had completed the eighth grade in that one-room country school, they called it a commencement. When I finished the Long Island, Kansas, high school, again they called it a commencement. When I completed graduate school in Illinois, again it was only a commencement. Likewise, when I complete my life on earth, it will be another commencement. The follower of Christ is always "reaching forth unto those things which are before."

Life's best road is one on which there must be concentration in prayer, study, thought and action. There must be cancellation, forgiveness of past sin with a willingness to come clean. There must be anticipation, the looking forward to good, the cheerful, and the best in this life and in the eternity with God. This is life's best road, and we have a right to it, knowing that nothing can cheat us out of our birthright. When we take every step with Christ, we will find all along the way the seed of goodness, that will ultimately struggle into flower and fruit.

PRAYER: O God, our Heavenly Father, we thank Thee for calling us to follow Thee on life's best road. Help us to live each day in an atmosphere of goodness and love that we may attract others to follow Thy best road. Amen.

9. HOW TO FILL THAT EMPTY FEELING

". . . I am with you alway, even unto the end of the world"
(Matthew 28:20).

THIS CHAPTER HAS BEEN INSPIRED BY THE THEME OF A
recent youth conference in which I was involved. The theme was
"Loneliness," or, as it was sometimes stated: "To fill the emptiness."

"Are young people lonely?" some may ask. Josephine Lowman,
a human relations advisor, who corresponds with many people of
all ages, said in one of her columns: "I have often thought that if
all the lonely people could get together at a national meeting, it
would probably be the largest gathering in the history of the
world."[1]

Loneliness, that empty feeling, is not a respecter of age, sex, or
environment. Probably some of the most lonely people in all the
world are boys and girls in some of our most crowded cities. I recall one young man's saying that the loneliest day in his whole life
was a Christmas day he spent in an apartment in New York City
with his dad who was divorced from his mother. He had gone to
the big city. There were people all around him, but he was lonely.
Loneliness is not always just being physically alone, but is often
a lack of something within one's self, a dreadful empty feeling.

The United Presbyterian Church has produced a little pamphlet
in their "Living Faith" series, called: "Why Be Lonely?" In it are
listed seven kinds of loneliness. They are: "The Loneliness of
Bereavement," "The Loneliness of Non-conformity," "The Loneliness
About the Hearth," "The Loneliness of Adolescence," "The Loneliness of the Single Adult," "The Loneliness of Older People," and
the most bitter of all, "The Loneliness of Sin."

Commenting upon some of these, it is stated concerning the
loneliness about the hearth: "The home can be a colony of heaven,
or an outpost of hell." The pamphlet points out that old age is the
most lonely age, but that the teenager is the second most lonely

[1]*Rockford Morning Star,* Rockford, Illinois.

person, for "The teenager is neither a child nor an adult. He is trying to find out who he is."

Finally, concerning the loneliness of sin: "If sin is fundamentally turning away from God to go our own way, the loneliness of being separated from God is obvious." The loneliness of being without God produces an agonizing God-shaped vacuum in the soul that cries out for something that will satisfy the craving to be filled with friendship and fellowship, like a thirsty man in Death Valley would cry out for water.

Loneliness is often the result of a lack of noble purpose for life. Concerning this frustration and loneliness, someone once said there are three things for which all men search and hunger. They are: "to be at peace with himself, to feel that life is meaningful, and that one's role is important in the divine scheme of things. . . . To be at peace with his neighbor—to enjoy the understanding, approbation and love of other men. . . . To be at peace with God—to know His love and infinite wisdom."

When you think about it, you find that every meaningful thing we yearn for does fall into these three categories. Most of the misery, misunderstanding, *loneliness,* and frustration that we must all battle at times comes when we are out of tune with ourselves, our fellowmen, or our God.

Loneliness, that empty feeling, we all have it. But, what can be done about it?

I.

Develop a right relationship with yourself. Do not be constantly at war with yourself. This happens more than we realize, and often we do not even know what is taking place. Perhaps we have done a great, or minor, wrong (if there is such a thing as a minor wrong), and we are torn to bits within because of the memory of it. God forgives and very often family and friends will forgive, but we are unable to forgive ourselves. Thus we continue to live with the bitter memory and the burning sting.

Such a feeling constantly drains off our energies, and we feel emptied of all goodness. As a result we are filled with guilt and are constantly kicking ourselves around. We have a little war going within ourselves. Such is a part of the loneliness of sin. When God and others forgive us, we must learn to forgive ourselves and start from there if we are to conquer this lonely, empty feeling.

Sometimes that wrong relationship with ourselves is because we take ourselves too seriously, a kind of locked-up-in-self loneliness. Again we sometimes do not recognize the problem with which we are afflicted. It has been a difficult day, and you fear that you will face another one just like it. With such thoughts you come home tired, thinking these thoughts, wondering why the people here, and where you work have to be so unfriendly, so mean and disagreeable. "They do not treat me right. I am being persecuted. I think I will move away from here and get into a community and a job where I am treated right."

You will always have that lonely, empty feeling unless you can change the relationship you have with yourself. You are too locked up within yourself, and that is a very lonely place to be. You cannot solve the problem by moving because you are the basic problem. And when you move you take yourself with you. Someone has wisely said: "I have to live with myself, so I want myself to be fit to know."

Learn to know yourself at your worst and at your best and be able to distinguish the difference between the two. Seek to develop your best by obtaining full forgiveness of your worst. Come out of your shell of thinking mainly of self. Give of yourself to the good of others.

II.

Develop a right relationship with other people.

Is your life empty, and are you lonely because you lack friends? Do you have an away-from-people kind of loneliness and would like to have more friends around you, those who have confidence in you?

Some of us are lonely because we are lazy about making the first move toward friendship. We always wait for the other person to take the first step. This may deprive us of many good friends. Perhaps that person you would like for a friend will never be a close friend if you do not take the initiative. It may not be because he has not been friendly enough to you. Do not be afraid to show your friendliness and your desire to have friends and be friends.

Let your friendship with others be genuine and communicate the fact that you are interested in them and not in getting something. I heard about one fellow who was overly zealous in obtaining a certain fellow for a friend. After he was sure of the man's friendship, he asked: "Didn't you tell me you would be my friend to the end?" He then said to his new friend: "That's great. Will you lend me five dollars?" To which the man quickly replied: "This is the end!" Sometimes we may not have friends because we tend to communicate a scheme to obtain something other than true friendship.

In the development of a proper relationship with other people, you will not only want to develop a friendship, but become helpful to people. You will want to be a friend and a helper to the friendless and those who cannot do for themselves and others. One of the finest ways to fill that empty feeling is to pour out all you have in helping others.

The rich young ruler went to Jesus one day and inquired as to how he might achieve the good life and establish right relationships with God and His kingdom. Jesus replied that the ruler should sell all he had and give it to the poor.

Here was a man of wealth with a lonely empty feeling, and Jesus counseled him to pour it into the helping of others. Here is a principle, given by Jesus, for filling that empty feeling. Sometimes, we will want to pour out of our friendliness toward the friendless, laboring for the good of others, assisting in the healing of the sick, teaching and helping in the mission of the church in bringing others to God, and giving of our resources to others. When we take the first steps of friendship and do these things, we begin to establish right relationships with other people, and this will help to fill the emptiness of our lives, and effect the cure for loneliness for both ourselves and others.

III.

Above all else, develop a right relationship with Christ by accepting Him as Saviour and making Him Lord of your life. Your right relationship with Him will be the best motivation for establishing the right relationship with yourself and others.

Man's natural relationship with himself, others, and his God has been somewhat strained from the beginning of the human race. After their first sin in the Garden of Eden, Adam and Eve suddenly found their relationship with themselves, each other and God something less than it should have been. As a result, they had an empty feeling and went away, hiding themselves in loneliness, so that when God came into the Garden, He called out: "Where art thou?"

Sin is the chief cause of loneliness of all kinds. A personal relationship with Christ as Lord and Saviour helps us conquer the problem of sin and find the forgiveness we all need. Therein lies the hope for right relationships and the cure for loneliness.

All through the Old Testament God was calling man back into right relationships and was seeking to get man to want to live righteously out of an inward love for God. The psalmist calls our attention to the essential, basic spirit of all right relationships with his poetic words: "I delight to do thy will, O my God; yea, thy law is within my heart" (Psalm 40:8). However, it remained for the coming of God in Christ to give us the motivation for such delight in the will of God that we can more easily establish right relationships. This Christ, whose life was so perfect, who had Himself conquered loneliness, and lived the full meaningful life because of a perfect relationship with the Father, has said to us: "I am with you alway, even unto the end of the world." Speaking of this Christ of meaningful life and living, the Apostle Paul has said: "The love of Christ constraineth us," or controls us.

It is comforting to know that this Christ is always with us. Therefore, let us come into proper relationship with Him, and let His love and goodness, as revealed in the Scriptures and by His spirit control us, moving us then into right relationship with ourselves and others. With His presence working within us and guiding us into the good life and the good relationships of life, our lives need never be empty, and we never need be lonely.

First of all, establish a right relationship with yourself. The first step here is to find the forgiveness of God by accepting Jesus Christ as Saviour. Then seek the forgiveness of others. Lastly, forgive yourself and be free of loneliness and guilt.

Secondly, establish a right relationship with other people. Loneliness is usually interpreted as a moving away from other people, or they from you. Move toward them and perform some good deed for one in need, and in the act of relieving his ache and loneliness you have relieved your own through this proper relationship.

Finally, establish a right relationship with Christ as Lord of your life. He is the perfect guide, the highest motivation, the closest friend, and He has promised: "Lo, I am with you alway, even unto the end of the world." He is the one who will help establish and re-enforce all other proper relationships. In doing so, He is the real cure for loneliness and the giver of the fullness of life. This is all made possible by His great shepherd heart, which understands our loneliness and leads us into the fullness of life daily. Give yourself to His shepherding care and be no longer lonely. This is how to fill that empty feeling.

PRAYER: Great God of our fathers. Thou who dost understand our loneliness, we do come to Thee for the fellowship, the companionship, the meaning which we can find in Christ, and for guiding us into the richness of fellowship with one another. May we, in Thy love, be friendly, considerate and more worthy. Amen.

10. HOW TO MASTER FEAR

"And the angel said unto them, Fear not: for, behold, I bring you good tidings of great joy, which shall be to all people" (Luke 2:10).

YOU HAVE NOTHING TO FEAR. IS THAT NOT A WONDERFUL and reassuring thing to know? Christ has come to earth that He might calm our fears. When He first came that night long ago in Bethlehem, the angel said to the shepherds: "Fear not." Christ has been saying: "Fear not" to all of us ever since. Yet, until we can fully grasp the impact of the spirit of Christ upon our lives, we have our fears. Man, without this reassuring message of the divine has always been fearful. Fear is one of the most deadly things welling up from within us. It is paralyzing human lives, demoralizing character, destroying ambition, reducing happiness and hindering noble achievement.

Much of this fear, the human race has brought upon itself, and has passed on from generation to generation. From birth, we are trained to be fearful. The child is cautioned a hundred times a year to look out for this and to flee from that. It will get bitten, poisoned, or killed, if it does not do thus and so. My sister tells about being in a restaurant at one time when the parents of a little child told the little one to sit still and be quiet because if he didn't the waitress would bring a sharp knife and cut off his ears. No wonder we have our fears. We are filled with them from childhood on up.

Many men and women cannot bear the sight of a little harmless insect or animal because they were told by someone in childhood that it would harm them. The adult who never makes a move, or allows the children around him to make a move, or do anything without parading a long list of terrible potential fears is embittering the young life with a deep-seated poison. Many of our greatest criminals are those who were taught to be fearful in childhood.

Fear, as an instinct, has its place. When there are real dangers like boards with nails in them, sharp glass, rushing traffic, a swift stream, or fire, we must be cautioned to be careful. We must have a certain amount of fear of the real dangers that sometimes lurk near. However, most of our damaging fears are not related to the real and obvious dangers.

The fears of many people stem from the fact that, as little children, they were confronted with unreal, fanciful fears. "Now if you don't be good, the ghost or the boogie-man will get you." "If you don't quit playing with those boys, that policeman out there on the street will come in here and hit you with his big club." I have heard of parents and baby sitters telling little children, in an attempt to get them to go to sleep, "If you don't go right to sleep a great big bear will come and eat you up." Let me ask if this were really true, how much sleep as an adult would you get in a situation like that? All such talk is entirely foreign to the spirit of Christ, and He came to tell us, "Fear not."

Consider how these unrealistic fears are carried over into adulthood. Go into almost any group, no matter how gay and happy the gathering may seem to be, still you will find that the cancer of fear gnaws at the heart of many present. There is the fear of accident, of sickness, of poverty, of the stock market, of death, or some terrible misfortune. On the surface, many appear to be gay and happy, but deep within they are living under the shadow of fear, haunted by the dread of some vague, potential, impending evil.

When Jesus came, the shepherds were told: "Fear not. . . ." (Luke 2:10). Later, in his ministry, Jesus said: "Fear not, little flock. . ." (Luke 12:32). At another time: "Fear ye not, therefore, ye are of more value than many sparrows" (Matthew 10:31). This was just after He had told them that not one sparrow fell without God knowing it. Then, after Christ had been crucified, the angel came to the women who were looking for His body, and said: "Fear not ye. . ." (Matthew 28:5).

Now we discuss the dark fears that stalk within our personalities, and expose them to the light of how to master them in the spirit of Jesus Christ.

I.

The first step toward the mastering of fear is the understanding of the nature of our fears.

The one main thing we must recognize is that what we fear is that which has not yet come to pass. It is non-existent. Dr. Brougher, speaking of how many people fear the future, told of an old lady who, when she was asked how she felt, replied: "I feel better. But when I feel better, it scares me, for I know I will feel worse."

Mark Twain once said: "I am an old man. I have had many

troubles, but most of them never happened." Not always, but many
many times the things that turn our hair prematurely gray and
plow early furrows in our faces, and rob the step of its spring and
take the bounce out of life are bridges that we never have to cross.
They are imaginary difficulties and misfortunes that never come.

Jesus cautioned again and again about this sort of thing when he
said: "Fear not, little flock." Also, He said: "Take . . . no thought
for the morrow: for the morrow shall take thought for the things
of itself" (Matthew 6:34). Jesus was not telling us not to plan for
the future.

The nature of many of our fears is an imaginary something that
we dream up, and which frightens us with its possibility. Suppose
one is afraid of polio. That is, one is afraid that he or some member
of his family will get it, suffer, and possibly die. So long as you are
imagining it will come, it does actually exist in the fearful state
which you fear. I know a lady who lives in a state of fear of the
imaginary. Whenever a member of the family arrives home late, she
meets him at the door in a state of hysteria, saying: "I just knew
you had a terrible accident and were killed," or, "I just knew
something terrible happened to you." Nothing of the sort has ever
happened to any of her family, but in her fears, it always has.

Indeed, the first step in mastering our fear is to understand that
most of what we fear never comes to pass, and is unreal as far as
we are concerned. Most people do not have terrible misfortunes
with which they cannot cope. Most people, along with Mark Twain,
have their troubles, but most of them never happen.

II.

*The second step toward mastering fear is the placing of confident
thoughts in the mind to take the place of the fearful thoughts.*

Merely convincing yourself that what you fear is unreal will not
be sufficient until you have learned to combat the fearful thought
with a positive thought. When the thoughts of foreboding fear
appear on the mental horizon with all their bigness and blackness,
not only should a person not indulge in them, but he should positively
change his thoughts in the opposite direction. In a sense there is a
comparison here with the word "repentance" as found in the Bible.
To repent of your sins means you, sensing the power of the Spirit
of God, personally turn from evil to Christ, following His leadership
and Lordship. If you have been in sin, turn from it and go in the
direction of righteousness. Similarly, a person can repent of his
fearful thoughts, turn from them, and move into positive, bold
thoughts. When fearful thoughts come, say with the psalmist, one

hundred times a day, if necessary: "The Lord is my light and my salvation; whom shall I fear? The Lord is the strength of my life; of whom shall I be afraid?" (Psalm 27:1).

If you are fearful of disease or personal failure, instead of thinking how weak, little, or inadequate you are in the face of it, think of ways to prepare for it, of how strong, healthy and competent you can become. You may not become everything you have wanted to be, but you can become everything God wants you to be. That should be good enough for anybody. The tragedy is that many become much less than what God had intended for them.

At first it may be a bit difficult to turn the current of thought from the depressing and fearful to the hopeful and confident, but with some help it can be done. Let none of us ever come to the point where we think we need no help with life's problems. We all do. To the person whose life is committed to Jesus Christ there is an abundance of spiritual resources and help. Let God help you get the hopeful and confident thoughts to replace the fearful ones. Remember the Scriptures, from beginning to end, tell of God saying: "Fear not." But there is then given the confident assurance of God's presence. Isaiah gives us the positive word of the Lord: "Fear not, for I am with you, be not dismayed, for I am your God; I will strengthen you, I will help you, I will uphold you with my victorious right hand" (Isaiah 41:10, rsv). Then a bit of good advice from the Apostle Paul of the New Testament that we have referred to while dealing with other themes, for it applies to all: "Whatsoever things are true . . . honest . . . just . . . pure . . . lovely . . . of good report; . . . think on these things" (Philippians 4:8). What better recipe can you find anywhere for the overcoming of fear?

Another positive course of action a person can take is the recalling of some humorous, pleasant, or interesting incident that means much to you. Also, read good books along courageous, humorous lines, and lines of noble interest. Catch the spirit of the one who said: "I would rather be the janitor of a sunshine factory than the president of a pickle factory." Spread sunshine and you will not have much to fear.

Another positive thing to do is to love everyone. John said, "Perfect love casteth out fear" (I John 4:18). Selfishness assumes right of ownership and possession of that which ought to be shared, and along with it comes the fear that we will lose it. Love does not demand, but gives and shares. "For God so loved the world that He gave. . . ." Since God gave, we need to give that others may have a good life as we have.

place some good, positive, confident thoughts in the mind in place
of the fearful ones.

III.

In the final analysis, I think much of our fear resolves itself in the
fear of death which must be faced and dealt with.

In this life, death will always be surrounded with a cloak of
mystery; however, a logical Christian understanding of it will remove the fear. It is one of the fears Christ came to remove. Said
He: "In my Father's house are many mansions. . . . I go to prepare
a place for you" (John 14:2).

The many stories we hear concerning ghosts and the cemetery
indicate that there is or has been a fear of death and the after
world. Dr. Ralph Sockman says that during his forty-four years in
the ministry no subject inspired more fears than death.

As to the act of dying, doctors will tell us that usually it is less
painful than many of the ailments we suffer while alive. It is like
going to sleep and waking up in another room. As Christians, we
believe in the resurrection. We believe we shall rise to be with the
Lord. He came that we "should not perish but have eternal life."
Christ is the one "who hath abolished death and hath brought life
and immortality to light" (II Timothy 1:10). "Fear not," He says.
"I will be with you." Most of our fears stem, in one way or another,
from our ultimate fear of death. But we need to understand that
in all of these we really have nothing to fear, not even in death, for
Christ has come, and is available in spirit to all who will receive His
spirit. Then, too, as His spirit comes into us, we are given the spirit
of hope and confidence.

The task of conquering fear is one of the most important tasks
you have. Not until this is effectively done can we take our God-
intended place and live the good life.

A little girl sat alone in a train, looking out of the window into
the ravine far below. A lady in the seat behind her asked: "Are you
not afraid?" Very quickly the little girl replied: "No, I am not. My
father is the engineer on this train." With confidence like that, have
faith in God, your Father, who is engineer of this orbiting world.
Fear not. God has come in Christ to bring good tidings of great joy,
which shall be to all people who will receive.

PRAYER: Dear God, give me freedom from fear, fill me with confidence, and the eternal home we have in Thee. Amen.

11. SELF-CONTROL OR EXPLOSIVE PASSIONS

"Be not hasty in thy spirit to be angry: for anger resteth in the bosom of fools"   *(Ecclesiastes 7:9).*

NO ONE CAN EXPECT TO ACCOMPLISH ANYTHING VERY GREAT as long as he is not king of his angry emotions. This is not to say that the one who is subject to frequent explosive outbursts cannot change and become a man of self-control, for he can.

Moses had this problem even after he was well on the way toward accomplishing his great work for God and his people. When he returned from the mount, having just received the Ten Commandments, he found his people worshiping a golden calf and dancing. Then that explosive passion of temper that had caused him to slay an Egyptian years before began to flame up within him, and he cast the tables of stone, with the holy commandments upon them, on the parched ground and broke them to pieces. He took the golden calf, burned it in the fire, and ground it to powder. The powder he then spread upon the water and made the people drink from it. The people had done wrong, to be sure, but it did not make it right for Moses to become inflamed with a passionate temper and break into pieces the stone plates. Moses was finally able to control this weakness and move forth to continue his great work. Unfortunately, this same lack of self-control has ruined multitudes of men possessing rare abilities, high ambitions and fine educations.

No group is exempt from this possible weakness of explosive passions. I knew a pastor who was an able thinker and speaker, a forceful, vigorous worker. Most of the time he was a warm, tenderhearted man who would do almost anything for anyone in need, and yet, he never found any great opportunity to minister because of an explosive temper. When someone in the church did something he did not like, or if a fellow minister displeased him, he did not hesitate to say from the pulpit just what he thought about him. Usually it was not pleasant. I was present at the time he was honored upon his retirement. After a few speeches expressing the traditional words of appreciation for his years of service, he was asked if he would like to take a couple of minutes to say something. He spoke twenty minutes and most of that time was taken up with bitter expressions and great outbursts of temper as he blamed one after another of the pastors and higher church officials for his not having had opportunities to serve the church in larger ways. It was evident from the manner in which he spoke why he had not been able to do more than he had.

A very hard-working, capable farmer I knew practically ruined his reputation and business because of his passion for telling everyone what he thought every time he became angry with them. When his temper was aroused, there was nothing too mean or too ugly for him to say. He would call people all sorts of names and rave without sense or reason. He drove his employees away from him and it was almost impossible for him to keep his men any length of time. I recall one time when one of his men asked him how to do a certain assigned task. The farmer flew into a rage and told him not to try it at all because in order to do that piece of work a person had to have brain cells. The man quit work and never came back.

When I was a boy I knew a girl who lived with our neighbors and not with her parents. One day when I asked why she lived with this family, I was told it was because of the explosive temper of the father. The mother thought it best that the little girl live elsewhere. Sometimes, the father, if he did not like something that was said would pick up a table-lamp and throw it through a window. He had been known, when he did not like the looks of the meal, to stand up and suddenly turn the table on edge, dumping all the dishes and food on the floor.

It is this type of behavior, in contrast to the kind of behavior God desires for us that we want to discuss in the next few pages.

I.

It has been widely believed, and perhaps accurately so, that a man in a fit of uncontrolled temper is really temporarily insane and possessed by demons.

In the syndicated newspaper column by the Duvalls, this statement was made for discussion, "An intelligent man will control his emotions!" Their discussion of it went as follows: "True, and by control we do not mean eliminate, but steer. Our emotions are like the motors in our cars. We do not want to cut them out, but rather to direct their power along constructive and long lasting channels. We do not know how to steer and how to accelerate."[1]

[1]"Let's Explore Your Mind." *Chicago Daily News.* October 8, 1962.

Notice that the advice is to "control," and not to eliminate one's passions and emotions. We need to keep that well in mind. However, no one is completely sane who cannot control himself. Rather, he is under the control of the demon that is in him. While in that state he would do things that he would regret the rest of his life. The following story illustrates how we are likely to do things we do not intend to do and do not want to say.

One day a man and his wife were arguing violently, and neither had much control of his temper any more, when the wife said: "I just wish I was not here with you. I wish I was in heaven." He, in his anger, replied: "I wish I did not have to put up with you. I wish I had a glass of beer." Then, in her uncontrolled, passionate fit of anger, she heatedly replied: "There you go again, always picking up the best for yourself." That is just about how much sense we make when we are under the control of violent emotions. In that state we not only say foolish and regrettable things, but we also do some very foolish and regrettable things.

I read in the newspaper recently about a girl who had, in a fit of anger, killed her boy friend. After it was all over, and she was in custody, she cried out: "It seems like a nightmare."

Many a person has to look back over a scarred and ruined life, a life filled with regret and humiliation because he had not learned to control violent emotions. "A man of great wrath shall suffer punishment" (Proverbs 19:19).

I once read about a family where the members were engaged in violent quarreling constantly. They would almost tear one another to pieces by their explosive tempers. Their faces would become transformed, and one could see the demons of passion flying and fighting there. This is a type of insanity that really need not be. If we start early enough, we can, with the help of God, overcome this illness. "Be not hasty in thy spirit to be angry" (Ecclesiastes 7:9). "He that is slow to wrath is of great understanding" (Proverbs 14:29).

II.

Uncontrolled emotions and passions in the mind changed the chemical composition of the various secretions in the body, developing poisons that eat away like foul acids, resulting in many kinds of bodily and personality damage.

Because the mental forces are so silent, we do not realize how tremendously powerful they really are as they work within the person.

Concerning these mental activities, think of how much a passionate explosion of temper will rob a person's entire system, mental and physical! Because of what this kind of activity does to a person, an outburst of temper will take more energy out of a person than a day's hard work. Some, after flying into a passionate rage, will tremble for hours afterward. These fits of anger will fill the system with poison just as much as the nicotine of a cigarette. They will work a great damage upon the body and mind.

Until recent years, and the thought still remains with many, we have been so accustomed to think of all forms of illness as the result of some disorder in the body that can be cured by drugs or surgery that it is difficult for us to look upon them as possibly caused by anger or violent emotion. Sometimes, we will remain angry for days and keep these poisons pouring into our systems.

There is no physical constitution or psychological mechanism in any human being so strong, but what it will ultimately succumb to the constant straining and twisting of the body and mind caused by an uncontrollable passionate temper. It takes only a few muscles to smile and a great many to frown. Every time one becomes angry, he reverses all of the normal activities that God has intended to be operative in a being, both physical and mental equipment. Think of what havoc excessive temper plays upon delicate nervous tissue, and of the interior deterioration of physical organs that is revealed in the wake of these tornadic passions of temperament.

Sometimes we are self-righteously in a kind of fit of anger. We constantly think of and call attention to the terrible things others are doing that we do not do. We say: "He smokes, and it is terrible," but we poison our blood with our anger over his smoking. We say: "He gambles away everything he has," but we wear away our very health with our anger over his gambling. We sometimes say: "He is killing himself with liquor," but we shorten our lives by burning them out with anger over his drinking. Occasionally we look at these things and get to feeling too angelic over our attitude toward them. If we are not careful, the world will look at us and say: "Yes, you are angelic all right, always up in the air harping on something."

There is something wrong with the "righteous" man if he cannot control his angry emotions even in the midst of the world's evil. The failure to exercise self-control will result in unhappiness, broken health, poor relationship with people and a premature death because such works wax evil upon the mind, the body, and all our relationships of life. This lack of control need not be; God has not intended that it be that way.

III.

On the positive side, which we now wish to emphasize, the Creator has made available to every person a divine power that is more than a match for his passion or vicious emotion.

If we will only pray to God with the psalmist: "Deliver me, O Lord, from the evil man: preserve me from the violent man," and seek to use all power available to overcome our evil and violent passions, we need not be a slave to our emotions. Said the Roman writer Horace in one of his epistles: "Anger is a momentary madness, so control your passion or it will control you."

The assurance from our Lord is that we can be in control. In Proverbs are some words of wisdom concerning controlling emotion. "He who is slow to anger has great understanding" (Proverbs 14:29, RSV). Also, "He who is slow to anger is better than the mighty, and he who rules his spirit than he who takes a city" (Proverbs 16:32, RSV).

Concerning what can be done in this area of control, it was reported that Horace Greeley acquired the habit of almost perfect self-control. He did not allow any threat, disturbance or disappointment inflame his temper. On one occasion it is reported that an angry reader called at the Tribune office and asked for the editor, Mr. Greeley. He was escorted into a seven by nine room where Greeley sat writing away at a rapid rate. The angry man asked: "Are you Mr. Greeley?" "Yes, sir. What do you want?" replied the editor without looking up from his work. The irate visitor began to upbraid him for an editorial that he resented. Mr. Greeley continued his writing without paying any attention to what the man was saying. After about fifteen minutes of the most violent scolding ever given a man, the angry visitor became disgusted because Mr. Greeley had said nothing, turned to walk out of the room. Mr. Greeley then looked up, rose from his chair, slapped the man gently on the shoulder, and in a pleasant voice said: "Don't go, friend. Sit down and free your mind. It will do you good. You will feel better. Besides, it helps me to concentrate on what I am writing. Don't go." The man left, but he was more disgusted with himself than he was with Mr. Greeley. Mr. Greeley had learned to assume the calm, deliberate, quiet, balanced composure which characterizes the good life as God intended that we live, and made possible for us to live.

An explosive temper is largely the product of false pride, selfishness, and cheap vanity. No man worthy of the name Christian will permit himself to be mastered by such passions.

Dr. James Whitcomb Brougher tells about driving his car south on Hill Street in Los Angeles one day as a big electric car was coming north. He forgot that it turned into the terminal in the middle of the block. Suddenly he woke up to the fact and stopped suddenly. The motorman stopped his streetcar with equal abruptness. When stopped, they were about two inches apart. The motorman stuck his head out of his cab window and shouted: "Where are you going, you old fool?" Brougher poked his head out of his car window, and, looking up at the motorman, said: "That's my name, but I didn't think you knew me." They both laughed, and Brougher said: "Sit still, and I will back out. I always back out when I get into a tight place like this." The motorman smiled, and said: "All right brother. You're a good sport." Dr. Brougher, commenting on this later, said: "That was better than getting mad and having a fight, and giving the newspapers a sensational story about the fighting between the minister and the motorman." By self-control, Dr. Brougher was the winner. Had he lost his temper and sought to retaliate, he would have been the loser.

The man who has learned the secret of self-control, mastering his angry passions, has learned how to protect himself from his mental enemies as well as his physical enemies. The one who has acquired this control over explosive passions has acquired the very essence of noble character. For one to be able to look a man straight in the eye, clearly and deliberately, without the tornadic ruffles of temper beginning to stir under extreme provocation gives himself a sense of victory which nothing else can give. To feel that one is master of himself in a delicate, tense, and explosive situation gives a dignity and strength to character, braces one and supports him on every side as nothing else can. "Be not hasty in thy spirit to be angry. . ." (Ecclesiastes 7:9).

PRAYER: Dear Lord and Father, forgive my feverish ways. Clothe me in humility and self-control. I thank Thee for Thy divine guidance and control, so available when we are ready to follow Thee and dedicate ourselves to Thy service. In Christ's name, the master of all self-control, I pray. Amen.

12. THE POWER OF LOVE

"God is love; and he that dwelleth in love dwelleth in God, and God in him" (I John 4:16).

THE STORY IS TOLD OF A YOUNG MAN WHO CAME HOME after a few years of service in the army. As he approached the old home in the hills, he looked sadly at the family farm. The place was terribly run down. The house needed paint, and the other buildings were falling apart. Fences were down, and the entire farm was a picture of decay and despair. As he looked over this place which had been his home for years, he said to himself: "Somebody has got to love this place." Indeed, that is what it takes if you want to improve something or somebody. You have to have the power of love. The power of love will transform a home and it will transform a life.

Knowing something of the power of love, and having heard the testimony of the ages concerning it, how strange, for example, that a young musician will spend hundreds of hours practicing and training a voice, and that a young man will devote years of hard study to the mastering of a profession or business, and that an artist will spend two decades learning how to paint a picture, and that an author will devote a lifetime to the production of one book, yet be unwilling to spend any considerable time learning how to love God and his fellow man.

The Scriptures teach us that God is love, and that he that dwelleth in love dwelleth in God, and God in him. Where can one find a greater power than that? With God dwelling in us we can have all the power, control, and influence that we ever need. This is the power of the love of God, and it can be ours. Yet, we see people hating, scheming, working early and late, sacrificing the best years of their lives trying to mass together a few thousand or a million dollars.

We seem to think real power comes from massing our millions. A hoodlum recently came to our city and was soon arrested. He told the officers: "You can't put me in jail. I'm worth a million dollars."

74

Nevertheless, he was put in jail.

There are places and situations where the power of money will not reach. However, the power of love will give one a wholesome, poised, well-developed sense of values and character that will protect him and insure his serenity and inner strength, no matter what losses and misfortunes might overtake him.

With love in a person's heart, he can look upon others with a great deal more tolerance, understanding and discernment. This will make him happier, make others happier, and further him on the pathway to successful living and the good life. Hate can never do this, but the power of love always can.

Of course, we are not discussing love in the narrow limits of romance as we so often think of love. In the narrow romantic sense we are not always sure what love is. Sometimes it is emotion, or fantasy. A fellow was once asked if he had ever fallen in love. "Yes," he replied, "about two years ago I met a girl, and it was love at first sight." "Why didn't you marry her?" asked the inquirer. To which the fellow replied: "I took a second look." A second look is always in order to determine whether or not it is real love.

In this chapter we define love and discuss the power that comes from practicing the love of God as He intends we shall.

I.

Let us define what we mean by love. In defining this word translated "love" in the English language, let us take a look at three background Greek words from which the English word is translated. *Eros* means an erotic, sensual type of love. *Phileo* is an intimate emotional affection, the kind of love which exists between husband and wife, parent and child, friend and friend. Neither of these are words used to denote the love we are emphasizing in this chapter. They are too narrow. They are not in total conflict with the greater love of which we are speaking, but they are not that kind of love.

Agape is the word we are looking for, and it means an attitude and disposition of good will toward others, even our enemies. Being *agape* and not *eros* or *phileo* does not mean we will rush to everyone we love and embrace them, kiss them, extend romantic, family affection toward them. However, it does mean we will wish for them the very best, pray for them and help them to achieve the highest good possible. This kind of love does not have to be sparked by attraction, beauty, or good works toward us. With the love of God in us, it can be launched by and controlled by the will, our reason, and imagination. This is the love of which we speak, and it has power.

II.

Training in love should begin very early in life. It is always easier to train the tender shoot, to make it grow in the desired direction, early, when it comes up through the soil. Think of how much this training means to the loveliness and beauty of a future tree. Also consider how much this training means to the future success of the young athlete. Likewise, realize how important it is for fathers and mothers to train the young mind in the ways of love, to turn the little mind from all its many enemies, from worrisome, fearful, despondent and sick thoughts. When that little one makes a friend of someone of another race or of another family with whom you have had trouble, do not poison the child's mind by sowing seeds of hatred. By sowing such hatred, you cripple, wound and limit the power of love. God has designed your child to love everybody, and the chances are he will if you, or someone, do not prejudice his thinking.

In the home, the vocabulary we use, the books we read, the attitudes we share that go beyond words all have a part in shaping our children to go out into the world to either love or hate. How important it is that we help the child select those words and build within his mind those images and concepts which make for love, joy, light, peace, comfort and happiness.

Sad to say, many people have not developed hearts of love. Many are indifferent to others' needs and desires. They are robbed of a power they could have. Yet, we can develop a love toward those who do not love. We need not let their lack of love rob us of the power of love. We cannot get everyone to love us, but they cannot keep us from loving them. Will Rogers, who said he had never met a man he didn't like, on one occasion found his car stalled in a mud hole. A man with a big car came, but turned aside and kept on going without offering to give a lift. Did Mr. Rogers become angry? Hardly! He only remarked: "If that is the milk of human kindness, I'll take mine from a cow." Will Rogers, who loved everybody, who could turn everything into something good or see the humor of it, was a man of power, far greater than a hating Hitler or a satanic Stalin with all their military might.

Not many rise to the height of a Will Rogers in their love for mankind, and not many sink to the depths of a Hitler or Stalin in their hate. Most of us find ourselves with a strange mixture of both love and hate in our hearts. We have probably received a little of both from our parents and families.

III.

Regardless of the degree of love or hate we possess, we can right now make the kind of changes in our hearts and minds that will put more of the love of God into our personalities. Some have grown up in a home where there was prejudice and hatred toward those of other races. Some have been taught that one must hate his enemies. But Jesus said: "Love your enemies." If we want the love of God to dwell in us we must love our enemies. Jesus came to love, and by loving He showed a power that could be had no other way. His power was victorious over sin and even death.

Though we may still be shackled by petty prejudice, bias, or hatred, we can shed these old weaknesses and find new life and power in the love of God. This love and concern for others will give you new power and greater happiness. A famous New York pastor tells about a husband and wife who drove all the way to the pastor's farm home that they might talk with him alone. The pastor said he was quite surprised for he had always thought of this man as a playboy of the ultra-sophisticated type. The man had tremendous artistic talents and was of keen intellect, but had never shown any sign of seriousness, earnestness, or depth. The man's wife, a rather elegant lady, seemed to be under great strain.

Very soon after they were seated in the pastor's study, the troubled man began to speak in a serious tone, saying: "We have come in the hope that you will guide us into a more satisfying way of life. My wife is sick most of the time, and, while I am well physically, in a different way, I am just as miserable as she. My life just does not count for anything. We are not happy, and we thought you might be able to help us."

This pastor was so surprised that he replied: "Frankly, I doubt that I can help you. You may be too sophisticated for my simple ways." Then he added: "But I can tell you where you can get help." "Oh, you want to refer us to someone else?" asked the man. "I want to refer you to the Bible," answered the pastor, "but I wonder if you have what it takes to try it. Frankly, I doubt that you do." Then he asked the couple this question: "Can you be simple and humble enough to give it a real try?" They both looked startled, and the man asked: "Why do you say that?" "Because your usual approach to life seems superficial," replied the pastor. To which the man so correctly replied, "That is a cover up for our frustration."

The pastor then outlined for them a course in Bible reading, steering them to passages filled with the love of God—the Psalms, the four gospels, and several of Paul's letters.

The couple was determined to turn from their old ways and truly find the love of God. And they did it. Later, in "lyrical, joyous expression," the pastor reported that the man wrote of the wonderful results. Said he: "Never has the grass seemed greener, flowers more beautiful, the sky bluer, sunshine more golden nor life more alive. Never have I had so much real joy and satisfaction in living. My wife's health is so much better that she is a different person." He then offered this final explanation: "God has come into our lives."

Remember I John 4:16: "God is love; and he that dwelleth in love dwelleth in God, and God in him." Their source of new life and power over old ways was the love of God that had come into their hearts through a surrender of their lives to Christ.

Your happiness will, likewise, depend to a great degree upon your ability to love. It does not make any difference whether you are a truck driver, a secretary, a teacher, a businessman, or the president of a large company. There is something different, radiant, and lovely about the person who genuinely loves. There are little touches of kindness here and there, a bit of good humor in the air, and a joyful life-giving radiance. You can have the good life of Jesus and the perfect love of God that He showed to us. Cultivate the bright, hopeful, uplifting, loving thoughts, and then make it practical by expressing them in all of your needs.

PRAYER: Great God of love, enable us to love the people with whom Thou hast placed us, and to love and give our best to Thee. Amen.

13. LIFE IS THANKSGIVING

"It is a good thing to give thanks unto the Lord"   *(Psalm 92:1).*

SOMEONE HAS SAID: "THE BOOK OF PSALMS IS THE KEY-board of the soul. It contains the whole music of the heart of man swept by the hand of his Maker." As Psalms unfolds in poetic beauty speaking to us about life, thanksgiving and gladness form the theme of many portions. Consider Psalm 23, Psalm 92, Psalm 100, and Psalm 103. Not a doleful note is sounded. Rather, we have: "Make a joyful noise unto the Lord, all ye lands. Serve the Lord with gladness: come before his presence with singing. . . . The Lord is good; his mercy is everlasting; and his truth endureth to all generations," etc. Truly, "It is a good thing to give thanks unto the Lord."

When we begin to live the good life, we begin to catch just a glimpse of the greatness and goodness of God. Our thoughts are turned to the exquisite language of the poet:

We see only a little of the ocean,
A few miles distant from the shore;
But, oh! Out there beyond—beyond our life's horizon,
There's more, there's more.

We see only a little of God's loving,
A few rich treasures from his mighty store;
But, oh! Out there beyond—beyond our life's horizon,
There's more, there's more.   —Author Unknown

Truly, the person living the good life will find that there is ever and always opening up for him just a little more of God's goodness, and he will feel joyfully constrained to live a life of thanksgiving for all these wonders of God's ever widening blessings.

When the Apostle Paul listed the cardinal sins in his second letter to young Timothy, he included unthankfulness as one of them. The ugly life is the unthankful life; thanksgiving is the good life.

Jesus had an experience one day that illustrates the contrast between the thankful and the unthankful. He met ten lepers. Of course, they all wanted to be healed. He healed them. They then went their own way, but only one of the ten came back to show any appreciation. When one lives the really good life he doesn't forget God's favors so quickly. His entire life is a life of thankfulness for God's continual blessings.

Often when we are reminded that we should be thankful people, we begin trying to sum up by naming the things for which we are thankful. One girl who was at the time going through some trying circumstances told me how she decided one day to list on one sheet of paper the difficult evil things she was confronting and list on another sheet of paper the things for which she could be thankful. To her surprise the list of things for which she could be thankful filled the paper long before the other list. This is always the case, and it shows us that in all of life and at all times there are those things for which to be thankful. All of life is to be lived in the spirit of thanksgiving.

We will now discuss what I like to call the three R's of the thankful life. To be thankful is right, reasonable, and religious.

I.

It is universally right to live a life of thanksgiving.

The highest gift for which we should be thankful and the most universal gift to mankind is God's giving of Himself in Jesus Christ. He is the same yesterday, today, and forever. He is trustworthy and His love and forgiveness never change. His compassion is everlasting, and our changing needs find answer in the never-changing God.

It has been said that Abraham Lincoln for a time lived with a very devout but very ignorant deacon. One night the deacon aroused young Abe from sleep by pounding on the door and shouting: "Wake up, Abraham! The day of Judgment has come!" Lincoln jumped from his bed and looking from his window saw a great display of stars shooting this way and that. It was a fearful sight, but, before becoming too alarmed, he looked to the North Star and found it to be in its place. He looked for other stars and found them in proper position. The great Lincoln concluded that the universe was still quite universally solid and sound.

So it is with God. In a changing and frightening world, ours is a changeless God. He is universally right and holy. It is universally right that we should be thankful to Him.

In the Scriptures, we read: "Make a joyful noise unto the Lord, all ye lands" (Psalm 100:1). The trumpets of thanksgiving are not to be blowing only for ancient Israel, but for all mankind. It is true we have an official Thanksgiving Day with historical roots and associations that are distinctly American. However, the sweet song of thankfulness, unofficially and broadly speaking, is not a national solo, but rather is an international and universal chorus. There are thankful people in Japan, Germany, Africa and South America as well as in the United States. We are not the only thankful people on the earth, and we can be thankful that we are not.

The psalmist, in his universal emphasis on thanksgiving is just as prophetic as he is poetic. He knows, as we should, that at any time any land or any people can find that for which to be thankful, and can find many reasons for praise and song. Thomas Carlyle once said: "Give me a man who sings at his work."

"But, can the Russian find anything for which to be thankful?" you ask. Of course, he can! The Russian today can find that for which to be thankful, just like the ancient Israelite could in his day of captivity, and the German under Hitler in his time. Actually, everybody can give thanks to God that He is in control of the universe and will bring freedom.

Being a universally good thing to do, giving thanks is a practical thing to do. Not many really do it. That is probably why we have so much discomfort and complaining. Only one of the ten whom Jesus healed came back to say: "Thank you." That may still be the proportion who really give thanks. We have wars, rumors of wars, and problems about nine-tenths of the time. When will we learn that to be cheerful, to be thankful, to be loving, and to give are the right things to do? Good cheer, thankfulness, and deep appreciation as a way of life will bring the good life, with health of body and mind.

The great Scottish theologian, James Stewart, quotes the late bishop of Liverpool, Francis Chevasse, as saying: "Praise and service are great healers." "In other words," comments Stewart, "when life grows sore and wounded, and it is difficult to be brave, praise God; if it is hard to do, make yourself do it, and in the very act of praise, the wound will begin to heal! Sing something and you will rally your own heart with a song! . . . Praise brings the wounded back to life's firing line again." There you have it—the universal rightness and practicality of living a life of praise and thanksgiving.

II.

It is deeply reasonable to live the life of thanksgiving.

There is that great passage of Scripture that we often use as a call to worship in our churches: "Know ye that the Lord he is God:

it is he that hath made us, and not we ourselves; we are his people and the sheep of his pasture. Enter into his gates with thanksgiving" (Psalm 100:3, 4a). Now, if the Lord is God, and He has made us—His sheep—and provides for us—His pasture—is it not reasonable that we should enter into His gates with thanksgiving? Of course it is!

A visiting pastor of my acquaintance was attending a unique presentation of a program and appreciated it very much. The program had been conceived and planned by a man with whom he often disagreed. However, he liked the program, and so he expressed his appreciation and thankfulness for the fine presentation. Those words of thankfulness established an entirely new and constructive relationship between that man and the pastor. Was it not reasonable that he should express his thankfulness? Of course it was! It was practical, too. It did both men a lot of good.

The giving of thanks should not be limited to a season. It should be our daily life, for "praise is comely" and nothing heightens a man's stature more than bowing before a higher power. Think of some great person you admire. Would you not feel a little greater if you could just go to that person and speak to him, thanking him for something? When we go to the great God and bow before Him, we feel thankful and begin to recall some of His forgotten gifts. We discover new mercies. A sense of indebtedness to Him begins to well up within us and our words of praise become wings which lift us upward toward Him. Isaac Walton said: "God has two dwellings: one in Heaven, and the other in meek and thankful hearts." Now is it not reasonable that we should live the thankful life that brings man and God together? Of course it is.

III.

It is properly religious to live the thankful life.

It is not stuffy, prudish, or fanatical to be a person who gives thanks to God and others. It is properly religious. It is one of the finest things a Christian can do.

One practical way to get the religious aspect of giving thanks into focus is to just remember that disbelief in God and unthankfulness turn life sour, whereas faith and thankfulness put a song into life.

When the psalmist speaks of entering into His gates with thanksgiving and into His courts with praise, he is specifically referring to entering the temple to praise, or other appointed places of worship to offer thanksgiving. In this same spirit of praise and thanksgiving, the New Testament invitation is that we are found "Not forsaking the assembling of ourselves together" (Hebrews 10:25).

The really great people have seen clearly the relationship between the religious life and the good thankful life. Plutarch said: "The worship most acceptable to God comes from a thankful and cheerful heart." Worship God. Thank Him. Be thankful. When our heart is in right relationship with the great heart of God, we become thankful, cheerful people who show gratitude and live the good life.

While it is good to take time to count our blessings, thanksgiving is bigger than an inventory or an audit. It is a spirit among us, a fundamental attitude of life based on a right relationship with a creating, loving, Heavenly Father. It also includes a right relationship with all His children.

To live a good life of thanksgiving is truly right. We find that it is reasonable and it is properly religious.

In the calendar of the United States, there is one grand, glorious, official Thanksgiving Day. But in the calendar of the good life of God's children, every day is unofficially a Thanksgiving Day!

> Were thanks with every gift expressed,
> Each day would be Thanksgiving;
> Were gratitude its very best,
> Each day would be Thanks-living.
>
> —Chauncey R. Piety

PRAYER: O God, Thou hast given me so much. Give me one more thing: give me a thankful heart. Help me to live right, reasonable, and be properly religious. In the name of Him who gave all I pray. Amen.

14. HOW TO OVERCOME WEAKNESS

"My grace is sufficient for thee: for my strength is made perfect in weakness" *(II Corinthians 12:9).*

VERY FEW PEOPLE POSSESS ALL THE STRENGTH NECESSARY to do all the things they would like to do. All people who have marvelous ability and tremendous strength in certain areas of life will have their weaknesses in other areas. Sometimes we permit these weaknesses to loom too large, or allow them to deepen, and they cripple life, offsetting our strong qualities, causing our accomplishments to be dwarfed.

Sometimes we find those who will not admit to any weakness. This is not good because we all have our weaknesses. When we lack the strength to admit that we have them, that becomes a glaring weakness in itself. The most dishonest person of all at this point is the one who will admit to no spiritual or moral weakness. I recently heard about a lady in our city who claimed to be a perfect person. She said: "I do not have a wicked bone in my body. The devil does not give me any trouble like he does most people." She reminded me of the butler who complained to his proud boss that he was greatly tempted by the devil. His boss said: "You must be a very wicked man. The devil doesn't bother me." The butler responded: "When you go hunting, sir, and shoot into a flock of ducks, which one do you chase—the one you killed, or the one you crippled?" "I chase the crippled one, of course. I don't have to chase the dead one." Then the butler smiled, and said: "Sir, the devil knows you are a dead duck." The proud man's weakness was exposed quite fully.

How sad it is to have dragged through life some weakness or deficiency that could have been conquered. The weakness may be a small one, perhaps, and yet, if it cripples life in any way, if it hinders achievement, if it is a continual humiliation, if it submits us to a hundred embarrassments, and keeps us from moving forward in life, what a misfortune it is!

84

I know many people who are "giants" in possibility and potential, but permit themselves to be tied down by some little gnawing weakness. They may be shy about getting into the act of the good life, or they may be fearful of what people will think of them if they attempt to lead a group, a committee, or a project. Some are fearful of reading or speaking before an audience. Some have a weakness for getting started in the morning on whatever they are to do. Some have moral weaknesses that cause regret and remorse. Some, of course, have physical handicaps that cannot be cured or corrected. However, they can be overcome in our minds and spirits so that in spite of them we can live the good life. Remember, the Lord has promised: "My grace is sufficient for thee: for my strength is made perfect in weakness."

One evening I was on the program for "Handicaps United" in Chicago. There I saw a demonstration of strength—the overcoming of weakness. I saw a young man and young lady in their wheel chairs wheeling along side by side down the hall and laughing gaily. I saw young boys wheel their chairs down the hall as fast as they could, then grab one wheel so they could screech around the corner and say: "How is that for peeling the wheels?" much like one might do with an auto. I saw these people doing many things and heard them talk about the things they were going to do. I heard them describe their work and their hobbies and could see how they were becoming a success in many areas of life. I saw a group of people who had learned that the good life did not depend upon strength of arm, of leg, but of an inner courage turned into strength of heart and mind. Such courageous and determined people cause many of us to feel ashamed for the way many much lesser weaknesses have defeated us so often.

One need not drag his defeating weaknesses through life when a little common sense, a little more right thinking in developing new habits of thought and a drawing nearer to .the promises of God would soon remedy them or lift us above them.

I.

Get rid of all sickness brought on by imagination. Just as imagination can have a good, positive effect, so, likewise, it can have a negative effect. Many people become weak by dwelling upon the thought that they are peculiar, or deficient in some respect. Some people think they have inherited certain tendencies or pecularities from their parents or ancestors, and they are always looking for their appearance in themselves. Others are just sure that the kind of community in which they live, the weaklings with whom they have to work and associate will limit their ability to achieve. This is just the way to cause weakness to appear, for what we dwell upon and encourage in the mind we usually get. Thus we continually increase potential weakness by worrying about it and dwelling upon its consequences.

The great majority of these weaknesses and peculiarities are simply imaginary, or are exaggerated by imagination. They have been encouraged, nursed, and brooded over as possibilities so long that they become real to the sufferer. The cure lies in doing exactly the opposite: dwelling on the qualities of strength and goodness. Again call upon the good counsel of the Apostle Paul in Holy Scripture: "Whatsoever things are true . . . honest . . . just . . . pure . . . lovely . . . of good report . . . ; think on these things." Do not think your way into weakness, but rather use your powers of imagination to climb the tower of strength and goodness.

It is well for one to remind himself often that he is created in the image of God, and that a perfect being does not desire imperfections and weaknesses. Our weaknesses come, in a very real sense, because of the way we have recreated ourselves in sin. There can be no weaknesses that cripple and hinder, except as man produces them, for the Creator never gave them to us.

The creation account in Genesis gives us a picture of how God created man and what He desired for His children. However, we soon find man engaged in an act of disobedience through which, we might say, he recreated himself as a fallen being with all of the weaknesses that hinder and cripple the human family. Now, man is being called to turn back to God and become "a new creature in Christ" or that he can get victory over weakness and sin.

In both I Corinthians 16:13 and I Samuel 4:9, we read: ". . . quit you like men, be strong." How well this counsel from both the Old and New Testaments applies right here. Let us quit dwelling upon and nursing weakness in the imagination and start dwelling upon the things of goodness and strength and be strong. In Ephesians 6:10, the Apostle Paul counsels us to "be strong in the Lord, and in the power of his might."

The first thing we should do in the overcoming of weakness is to get rid of all weaknesses that are brought on by imagination.

II.

The second thing to do is to apply common sense to the real weaknesses you may have.

Consider once again the "handicaps" already mentioned. They are applying common sense to their natural weaknesses. Many of them are taking what has come to them in the spirit of Christ. I did not hear them whine, make excuses, take advantage of people, or even expect people to do a lot for them.

Give serious thought to your weakness, and with a godly, common-sense approach, conquer it or rise above it. If you have not had the opportunity to acquire the proper schooling and education that you would have liked, simply get busy and read and study. It is never too late to learn. Someone has said: "You cannot teach an old dog new tricks." Someone else said: "If that be true, it probably wasn't a very smart dog in the first place." However, we are not dogs. We are people, created in the image of God and always capable of learning. If it is not possible to acquire the learning we need for the things we want to do, we will have to adjust our lives to the things we can do. The making of this adjustment will, in itself, be a mark of strength.

If you have a physical weakness or handicap, you are in good company. The Apostle Paul had it. He referred to it as "a thorn in his flesh." He even prayed that it be removed. The answer to his prayer was that it would not be removed but that the grace of God would be sufficient to enable him to cope with it. It is comforting and reassuring to know that these weaknesses can be coped with, and that in spite of them one can, like the Apostle Paul, do great things.

The Christian, common-sense approach to the problem of our weakness is to remember that God has promised: "My grace is sufficient for thee: for my strength is made perfect in weakness." Thus, remember that God is near. Sin and weakness are condemned. Death is doomed. In spite of our weaknesses, life can have its royal second chance. Go to God with your problem, state your needs, explore the resources of your faith, live your love, and call upon His infinite everlasting power. The psalmist did this as he cried out: "O Lord, my strength and my redeemer" (Psalm 19:14). "The Lord is the strength of my life" (Psalm 27:1).

If you do not have any serious weaknesses, thank God for that. Then dedicate your strength to the helping of those who are weak. However, if you have inherited or acquired weakness through illness or accident, you will simply have to work a little harder to make up for it or to overcome and rise above it. However, with the help of God, it can be gloriously done.

In Frances Winwar's book, *The Haunted Palace,* we are told how Edgar Allen Poe was born of a drunkard and a morally frail woman. One of the reviewers says: "The color of his days was all but fixed before he knew their winter darkness." This has been true for many, but they have been able to rise above it. They have been able to fling open the shutters and let in the light of strength. The one who wants to be strong recognizes and admits his weaknesses; then, with the help of God, he climbs over them.

We have stated that, first, we will want to get rid of all weaknesses brought about by imagination; and, second, apply common sense to the real weaknesses we may have. This leads us to the third and more positive emphasis.

III.

Build within yourself the confidence that you can become strong.

We must beware of pride, however, at this point, by recognizing that this strength is not our own but it can come to us as a gift of God. Remember again the words of the psalmist who gave God credit for his strength to overcome. Let your confidence be in this spirit and the spirit of the Prophet Habakkuk, who said: "The Lord God is my strength" (Habakkuk 3:19). Let God build a confidence within you that will enable you to say with the Apostle Paul: "I can do all things through Christ which strengtheneth me" (Philippians 4:13).

With a Biblical foundation, with the promises of God, launch out into life, holding persistently in your mind the picture of strength, with a determination to possess this strength as your birthright. God has created us to embody His unfailing strength for the doing of His will in the world and for the helping of other people, which is His will. It will take a lot of courage to face the world and announce that in the midst of our normal human weaknesses God has placed strength. However, it can be done, because it can be true. There is a hymn that contains these words:

> Courage, brother, do not stumble,
> Though thy path be dark as night;
> There's a star to guide the humble;
> Trust in God and do the right.

The biographer of the Italian patriot, Garibaldi, tells of how one night a soldier in the great liberator's army was brooding outside his tent in the moonlight. His earlier strength and enthusiasm had faded into weakness. He was thinking of how he might desert and return home. Suddenly, the great commander came by. In a glance he appraised the situation. He seemed to read the weakening thoughts that were in the young soldier's mind. He laid his hand on the man's shoulder and spoke just one word: "Courage." That is what it took.

It will take courage for us, also, to overcome weakness, for courage is the foundation stone in the great structure of strength. God, in essence, said to Joshua, "Be strong and of a good courage and I will strengthen" (Joshua 1:6, 9). The great temptation today is to lose courage and become weak as we face the bigness and uncertainty of the future. However, we can overcome this weakness as we recall our Lord's words to His disciples in the face of similar uncertainties: "In the world ye shall have tribulation: but be of good cheer; I have overcome the world" (John 16:33).

Weakness, human frailty? We all have it to one degree or another, but we can overcome it and live the good life and do great things. Consider again the text: "My grace is sufficient for thee: for my strength is made perfect in weakness." To sum it all up in paraphrase, we can say: "The grace of God is sufficient for all of us, and His power is such that when working in us it will enable us to overcome all weakness." Therefore, let us freely admit our weaknesses and take them to Him. "My strength is made perfect in weakness." What a wonderful promise to any of us with a weakness or sense of inadequacy. God can and will bring out His strength in us, and He often does it at the point of our greatest weakness that we might know the deeper experience of His power and love enabling us to become strong in Him.

PRAYER: Great God of all strength, in the midst of weakness help us not to lose heart, nor hope, nor faith. When we feel our weakness, give us strength to overcome, to bear the stress and strain, and to possess a hope that will never fail and a faith that will bear all testing. Amen.

15. GOOD CHEER: GOD'S MEDICINE

"A merry heart doeth good like a medicine"   *(Proverbs 17:22)*

AT ONE OF OUR NATION'S MOST CRITICAL HOURS, ABRAHAM Lincoln called his long-faced, solemn cabinet members together and began to read to them a delightful chapter of humorous, cheerful nonsense by Artemus Ward. What? Humor at a time like this, they thought.

After a while Lincoln looked at the men, and asked: "Why don't you laugh?" He then went on to say: "With the fearful strain that is upon me night and day, if I did not laugh, I would die. You need this medicine as much as I do." Indeed, laughter, good cheer is God's medicine for us. "A merry heart doeth good like a medicine." Oliver Wendell Holmes once said that laughter was God's medicine, and everybody ought to bathe in it.

If people fully knew the health-giving powers of good cheer and laughter and practiced the continual expression of joy and gladness, a lot of doctors would be out of work. The cheerful man has a creative, health-giving power which the pessimist can never have. There is nothing that can so completely sweeten life, take out the drudgery and ease the jolts as a sunny, hopeful, cheerful disposition. Good cheer is the spiritual oil of gladness that reduces friction, anxieties, and disagreeable experiences. The mental, spiritual, and personality machinery of a cheerful person does not wear out or grind away like the one whose disposition is sour and disagreeable.

I.

Good cheer, a merry heart, is definitely one of Nature's greatest medicines.

God has created good cheer and laughter to bring the disordered functions of body and mind into harmony. I have had the experience of being tense for a few days because of problems that I faced: much work to do, or giving too much time to prolonged study and thought, until I found it difficult to sleep at night, and, as a result, did not feel well. I have also, at such times, in the midst of my tenseness, had the opportunity to attend a good humorous play, or spend an evening with some friends where there was singing, the telling of jokes, and laughing. When this happened, I would be able to go home, go right to sleep, and wake up fully rested the next morning. Good cheer really works.

The wholesome effect of good cheer, humor, and laughter is written right into the laws of the universe as God created it. It is often a cure for headaches, heartaches, and life's bruises. It helps to bring abnormal conditions back to normal. Furthermore, people who find greater physical and mental health and harmony through good cheer and laughter tend to live longer than those who constantly take themselves and life too seriously.

The superintendent of a home for the aged told me that when people came there to live, they seemed, as they mingled with others of their age who understood them, to become more cheerful, more given to laughter, tending to forget the cares of life and seemed to live forever.

In order to become more normal, more healthy, and live longer, the joyful forces within us must be released. Good cheer and laughter is one form of exercise that sets us free from the abnormal and rescues us from the blues.

There is no wonder drug that can compete with the wonder of cheerfulness. When I was about sixteen years old, I had the "flu" and the measles at the same time. I was very ill. When I saw the jolly, good-natured, cheerful doctor come into the room I began to feel better already before taking a bit of medicine.

"The power of cheerfulness to do good," says a great doctor of a generation ago, "is not an artificial stimulus of the tissues, to be followed by reaction and greater waste, as is the case with many drugs. The effect of cheerfulness is an actual life-giving influence throughout a normal channel, the results of which reach every part of the system. It brightens the eye, makes ruddy the countenance, brings elasticity to the step, and promotes all the inner force by which life is sustained. The blood circulates more freely, the oxygen comes to its home in the tissues, health is promoted, and disease is banished."

The teaching of Scripture and the Christian faith is that God is definitely interested in our well-being and health. I think much of Jesus' healing and health-giving effect on so many was due, at least in part, to His genuine cheerfulness. "Be of good cheer, I have overcome the world," He said.

"A merry heart doeth good like a medicine" (Proverbs 17:22).

II.

Good cheer is a very important characteristic in the successful life.
Many a person who could have lived the good life sleeps in a
failure's grave because he did not find the life that could lift him
above the routine of the dull, somber, and sour. When one permits
a sour disposition to master him, he then becomes the kind of person who poisons the atmosphere about him, and, as a result, his
relationship with other people becomes unhealthy, and his own
chances of social or business success are paralyzed.

A person simply must have good cheer and learn to get along
with other people if he is to be a success at life. It has been said
that a person can be very efficient at this job but be dismissed from
work if he cannot muster enough good cheer to get along with
those with whom he works. One does not become a cheerful person
just so he can become a business success. One does not say: "If
this is the only way to be successful, I will become cheerful, otherwise, I would choose to remain dull and somber. The cheerful life
has its other deeper, more eternal rewards. However, business and
social success are certainly products of the cheerful life.

A small newsboy one day sold a newspaper to a wealthy snob
who handed him a half dollar and said with a snarl: "Keep the
change and get some soap and water to wash your face." The boy,
quick as a flash replied: "Here, you take the change and go buy a
book on etiquette and learn how to be a gentleman." That man
was not a success with that little boy. He lacked the good cheer
needed and was too serious and pompous.

No one wants to become a close buddy with one whose personality has become stale, uninteresting and abnormal from not developing the cheerfulness that God intends that we have. To lack
friends, no matter how much money a person may have, is to be a
failure in the business of life. To fail in the flinging out of joy and
kindness wherever we go, and to try to keep all of life's goodness
and joy to ourselves, without sharing it, will pull us away from
people and doom us to a life of failure quicker than just about
anything else.

I once read about a man who led a very self-centered, selfish and
uncheerful life. He had no friends and no place to go on Christmas.
He would give no gift and would be receiving no gifts. On Christmas Eve, he accidentally locked himself in a vault with a time lock
that would automatically open the day after Christmas. At first, he
was not worried, for he thought: "Somebody will miss me and let
me out." But as he further thought about it, he realized that no-
body would miss him. No one missed him, and he spent Christmas

much as he lived, locked inside the vault of selfishness, dullness, and social somberness. All through the years he had lived so much to himself, without good cheer. No one was near to him, no one depended upon him, no one expected a gift or greeting. Without cheerfulness and friendship, he had made a practice of missing the Christmas cheer. Locked in a vault of money, probably his own, he was not a success in life because he constantly missed the joy and gladness of good cheer that is so necessary to the successful life.

III.

If we are to further enjoy the good life, we must pass this good cheer on to our children and coming generations.

We must encourage our children to be merry and to laugh aloud. It does one a lot of good to hear a child laugh. Do not be content with just a giggle or a snicker, but encourage the deep-throated laughter that comes from deep down within our being.

Just as you would train your child in reading, spelling, business, politeness, likewise, train him in the cultivation of cheerfulness. Of course, if you train your child in the art of wit and good cheer, it will come back to you rather sharply once in a while. Do not fear that too much. Be proud of him. One time a father told his boy that he should be studying harder. "Just remember," said the father, "when George Washington was your age, he was studying surveying and was already quite efficient at it." The boy quickly replied: "Yes, Dad, and I want you to remember that when George Washington was your age, he was president of the United States."

Listening to Art Linkletter's program recently, I heard him ask a small child what he wanted to be when he grew up. To which the boy replied: "My mother wants me to be a Methodist preacher, but I want to be a cartoonist instead." If he should want to be a cartoonist, let him be one. He can bring a lot of good cheer to a lot of people. Let us pass on to our children good cheer and encourage them to express it in the best, most wholesome way that they can.

True religion, the Christian faith at the best, is not chill and somber, but full of hope, sunshine, optimism, and cheerfulness. It is joyful, glad and beautiful. The Faith that Christ taught was bright and lovely, otherwise little children would not have flocked around Him as they did. Notice how the sunshine, "The lilies of the field," "the birds of the air," the hills, the valleys, the trees, the mountains, all had a part in the teaching. These are cheerful things shared by the founder of the joyful Christian Faith.

Some time ago, I was visiting with a man, and just as we were to part, not to see each other for another year, I said to him: "Keep cheerful." He looked at me with a surprised look on his face, and then finally said: "That's good advice. I am going to keep grinning whether I like to, or not."

That's it. Not just a grin, however, but a real smile of cheerfulness, come what may, and then the good will come. "A merry heart doeth good like a medicine."

PRAYER: Grant, Father, the Giver of all good cheer, there may be cultivated in me a reverence for and a greater appreciation of truth, beauty, and good cheer. Help me to share it with others that the world may become a better, more cheerful place in which to live. Amen.

16. PROCRASTINATION — HOW TO MASTER IT

". . . today I must abide at thy house"   *(Luke 19:5).*

Procrastination, the habit of putting things off, is a universal human weakness. We all have it. The most difficult part of writing that letter is getting started. The hardest part of studying for an examination in school, or preparing one's self for that new job is the getting started.

My father used to tell about how, before 1920, many people used to try to sell him one of the new Model T Fords that were on the market. However, he would see how many were having to seize the crank and spin it until they were exhausted before getting the car started. He would then say: "Someday, someone will invent a self-starter for these things. I will then buy one." In the autumn of 1921, he purchased a new 1922 Ford with a self-starter. All he had to do was press the button, and he was ready to go.

However, the self-starter for human beings is not so simple. It is largely, as someone has said: "The firm of Delay, Dally and Wait is one to which we all belong, and it is not far from bankruptcy most of the time." So often when we face our mountain of duty, we put it off. In the face of responsibility, we delay as long as possible.

Yet we dislike procrastination because it piles up work for the future, the way a flood piles up trash and debris, and the way a bulldozer mounds up surplus soil. It never solves anything. It only postpones it, and it eventually has to be dealt with. Lao-tzu, a wise man of China in 6 B.C., said: "The biggest problem in the world could have been solved when it was small." Very often, that which has been postponed becomes more difficult to deal with than it would have been at the proper time.

Our religious life and our relationship to God get caught in this massive web of delay. Very often, someone will say to me: "Pastor, I know I ought to be in church Sunday mornings, and I am going to get started soon." However, you can assume ten to one that he will not get started. He has been telling himself that for years, and 90 per cent of those who have fallen into this pattern never get started.

Several leading denominations have distributed to their churches a little leaflet, entitled: "Notice . . . Revision of Church Schedule." It deals with our procrastination habit in relationship to our church. The heart of it is as follows:

1. The pastor will save all his sermons and preach 52 on the last Sunday of the year. Be prepared to stay 23 hours.

2. The pastor will not make any calls, conduct any funerals, perform any marriages or baptisms till the last week. Please, arrange your weddings, illnesses, and deaths accordingly.

3. The choir will not sing until the last Sunday; then it will sing 52 anthems.

4. The janitor will not clean the church until the last week; but then he will do it 52 times so the building will be spotless on December 31.

5. Sunday school teachers are asked to write their own lessons, since we cannot afford to buy quarterlies.

6. The church and Sunday school will not be heated or lighted except during the last week of the year.

7. There will be no church bulletins until the last Sunday in December. On that day there will be 52 bulletins to inform you of what is going to happen during the past year.

8. There will be no work done for repair and upkeep until the last week. Meanwhile, pay no attention to the drafty cracks and the peeling paint.

9. The executive secretaries, department heads, field workers, missionaries, stenographers, etc., will stop eating and paying rent till the last week of the year. Their long rest will leave them in good condition to turn out a full year's work in the last week.

10. Retired ministers and widows and orphans will learn to do without food till the last week of the year. Then we'll stuff them with enough to last them till next December.

11. Seminaries, colleges, and mission schools will hold classes only during the last week of December. Some adjustment will be necessary here, as all the students will then be home for Christmas; but surely God will understand our situation and will provide some education for our young people.

Humorous? Even ridiculous? Of course! However, it speaks of the seriousness of our procrastination habit in our relationship to

God and His church. We put off attending church. We put off taking that office or that Sunday school class. We delay in making our commitment. We say: "Some day I will tithe, but not just yet." If only we could get started with these and other important things, we would be on our way to building churches and Christian lives with great creative power.

Jesus did not delay, dally, and wait when there was an opportunity to serve His Father and fellowman. One day a little man by the name of Zacchaeus desired to see Jesus. There was a great crowd around. Jesus was busy and could very well have put him off by saying: "Wait until tomorrow, or next week. I want to get some other things done first." However, this He did not do. Rather, Jesus said: ". . . today I must abide at thy house." Growing in Christ-like knowledge and grace, as well as mastering all situations of life would not be nearly so great a problem, if we could, *today*, make up our minds to get started doing the things we ought to be doing. Abraham Lincoln once said that a job was half done once you had gotten started.

Procrastination is the habit of delaying the good life for which we have all been created. It is the slowing of the advance of the kingdom and will of God. We come to the end of the week and then there is still that mountain of duty not yet scaled. Suddenly, we are at the end of the month, and then the end of the year, and things we had intended to do are not done. Sometimes we go through life and important things are not taken care of. Sometimes friends or relatives have passed on, and we have not done for them the things we had intended to do. We have not visited that kind aunt or that dear father or mother.

We can master this problem of procrastination and thus reduce the ravages, losses, and heartaches it brings to our lives.

I.

Break down your duties into manageable units.

Much of the delay in getting at our tasks lies in viewing them as massive, multitudinous and myriad of things to do that have suddenly overwhelmed us like a winter blizzard. We cannot see the snowflake for the snow. However, that is exactly what we must do. Break down that blizzard of things to do, into snowflakes, so you can handle it. At least get that snowbank of duty into shovelfuls. Many times I have heard people say, as have you: "I have so much to do that I don't know where to begin." The tragedy is that under such circumstances many of us do not begin. Our tasks are then left for someone else to do, or left undone. Some things are accomplished late and thus are less effective or less helpful.

When I was in graduate school, we were given the entire semester's assignment on the first day of classes. At that stage it looked like a mountain of duty, impossible to scale. The requirements for the semester might be: the reading of twenty books (large ones, too); the consultation of another fifty books in preparing a half dozen research papers. When we approached it in segments it did not look so insurmountable. Broken down, it went something like this: the reading of one book per week, the consulting of maybe a half dozen other ones at a time, and the completing of one research paper every two or three weeks. However, some of the students were still always behind and late with their work because they had not mastered the technique of breaking it up into manageable units and getting on with the job.

One time I said to a fellow who was always behind and late with his papers: "If I were always late like this, it would simply get me down." He replied: "It does get me down." Of course, it would, and it will get the better of anyone who will not break down his work into manageable units.

Recently I read about a new waitress who, after looking at a coconut cream pie, did not feel qualified to cut it into the proper, even-sized pieces for serving, so she asked the manager to help her. He simply picked up an aluminum pie divider and pressed it down onto the pie, leaving proper lines of demarcation. He then told her to follow the lines and cut the pie, and to serve it one piece at a time.

Like that, divide up your duties. Draw convenient lines of demarcation around that mountain of duty, slice your mammoth task into manageable segments and then complete them one at a time. It is called the military strategy: divide and conquer. The old philosopher poet said: "Life is hard by the yard; by the inch, it's a cinch."

II.

Get busy, quickly, and do those tasks that you have divided into manageable units.

You may have a thousand things to do next year, but now that you have them divided into only three a day, get busy and do the three each day as the day comes. This is the way to keep them from turning into six the second day, nine the third, and twelve the fourth day, and so on, ad infinitum, so long as one may procrastinate.

As you get at those tasks, now broken down into manageable units, undertake your more difficult units of work first while your strength and enthusiasm are fresh and full of vigor. Again, to refer to my experience in graduate school, the more difficult classes were scheduled to meet early in the day. Also, the professors always recommended that on week days and study days, we do our heavy solid reading early in the day while the energy of our minds was fresh and alert. I have found this to be good advice for all of life.

After beginning the day with prayer, I seek to get right at my more difficult tasks. I continue to devote my morning hours to the more heavy solid study and the areas of creativity. As the day wears on, I tend to shift to easier tasks, like answering mail, making telephone calls and pastoral calls, reading the newspapers, lining up business for coming meetings, etc. When I do this, I find that after tending to numerous easy tasks in the afternoon, I often get a second wind and can return to the more solid, creative study in the late evening hours.

Each one will have to analyze his own work and, after determining what is more important, more difficult, simply get at it and do it.

III.

Deliberately and purposely put yourself in the position of being compelled to do your work on time.

Plan a schedule, and to a reasonable degree, get other people and events into it in such a way that you simply have to meet schedules. The seasons of the year do this for us in many areas of life. The farmer who does not plant his crop in season simply does not reap. The man who fails to put anti-freeze into the radiator of his auto suddenly finds it frozen and possibly ruined. There are deadlines imposed upon us by society which, if we do not meet them, cause us to be left out, or behind. That train, that bus, that airplane simply does not wait. If a person wants on, he simply does not procrastinate beyond a certain point. If you are a student, you know that classes start at a certain time. If you are not there on time, you are marked late. School is not geared to our procrastination habits. We must gear our schedule to the school.

In the areas of life where you are the sole ruler, set up for yourself some schedules like that and follow them just as you would a bus schedule, or a school schedule. This will take a lot of self-discipline, but it will pay off with great dividends, and time will be saved with much more accomplished. This is the way busy people can get so much done. They build a schedule and let it rule them.

Build for yourself a reasonable worthy schedule and let it rule you. Your time is the life-blood of personal and corporate accomplishment. It brings you into life and brings life into you.

Remember what Jesus said, when He saw a little man in need of His help and fellowship: "Today, I must abide at thy house" (Luke 19:5). He did not say next week or tomorrow. He said, "Today." Jesus did not delay, dally, nor wait. He did not procrastinate when there were tasks he should be doing. He did not fret about the tomorrow nor the mountain of duty that stood a month away. He simply confronted each day as a segment of time and duty and did what He should.

Say to yourself: "I have taken Jesus as my Master; I will be a follower of His. I will break down my mountain of duty into manageable segments. I will then get at the tasks that lie before me. I will exercise some self-discipline and compel myself to do the things I ought to do and do them on time.

PRAYER: O God, the Father of all time and eternity, I bow before Thee in quietness and in confidence, knowing that in Thy strength I can be ready for the tasks with which I have been matched. Give me the grace, the courage, the ability to start my tasks where I am, and move on to where I ought to be. Amen.

17. HOW TO MASTER WORRY

"Rejoice in the Lord alway: and again I say, Rejoice"
(Philippians 4:4).

A DOCTOR HAS SAID THAT 70 PER CENT MORE PEOPLE OF the world, who are sick, would recover sooner if they did not worry so much. Someone else has said it is profane to be a religious person and worry excessively, for to worry is to deny your faith. Indeed, genuine faith helps to rejoice and not to worry.

Of course, worry is not altogether bad. The psychologists tell us that worry is one way the mind can protect itself from anxiety. What is anxiety? "Anxiety is worry without an object." Our minds and spirits, when anxious, try to find an object, and when an object is found, we find a certain amount of help for at least then we know what it is that is bothering us.

Worry and anxiety are related, however. The word, "worry" and the word, "anxiety" come from the same root word, which means "to choke or strangle."

Worry does have the effect of reducing the free expression of our powers. Some have called worry the "universal sin." Others have referred to it as "the great American disease."

Men fill their lives with business and professional worries, and women fill their lives with home and social worries. Young people are worried about grades and popularity. However, Jesus said: "Be not anxious for your life, what ye shall eat, or what ye shall drink; nor yet for your body, what ye shall put on" (Matthew 6:25, ASV). On the more positive side, the Apostle Paul said: "Rejoice in the Lord alway, and again I say, Rejoice."

All of us have the two sides of life: the worrying side and the rejoicing side. Consider, for example, a day in which early in the morning you feel happy, and you do not know why. You are laughing and you are singing. Suddenly, you ask yourself: "Why am I so happy today?" Then you suddenly recall: "Oh, yes, we are going on a picnic with a dear friend who is coming." Or you received that tax refund check the day before. You think of something lovely that has happened or expect to happen, suddenly recalling it to your conscious mind. Your conscious mind had forgotten it for a while, but your subconscious had not forgotten it; therefore you had an attitude of happiness.

On the negative side you may have the same kind of action. In this case it will be anxiety. You start out in the morning feeling sad, down-hearted, and mournful, and you do not know quite why; but, if you are fortunate, you will be able to look around and inside yourself, or you look on your schedule of events, or suddenly you recall something that happened or that you expect to happen. Then you can say: "That is why I have been anxious and tense." At that point, your anxiety is changed into worry.

The next step you take is: Let worry be changed into confidence in God. The Lord wants you to take that step, so that, instead of being anxious or worried about tomorrow, you will be able to rejoice in the Lord.

One lady, when she thought she had the weight of the whole world on her shoulders, was counseled to budget her worries. Specifically, she was told: "If you want to worry, go right ahead and worry, but worry fast and put things on a business basis. Make out a worry budget. Plan so much of your day for worrying, and when your allotted time is up, drop it until your next worry period. Turn everything over to God while you are about other things." She reported that it was a startling idea, but upon trying it found it to be wise counsel.

I read about a lady who had six children of her own and then took in six more children to rear. Someone went to her and asked: "Why do you seem to be so unperplexed? You seem not to have a trouble in the world. You are gay. You are happy. You are glad. You have a kind of enthusiasm that communicates itself to other people. How does this happen?"

She replied: "It happens like this: I go to God and say: 'God, I will take care of the work if you will take care of the worry.' It has never failed, because the work has filled my time, and God has faced the worry."

We will worry, but in keeping with the worry budget idea, let us not be a spendthrift with it. Live within the worry budget, and let God, the silent partner, carry the larger portion of the load as He wants to do. He has an inexhaustible supply of ideas and techniques that will help us rise above the worrisome tangles of life.

What are some definite, God-given techniques by which we can begin right now to help us master worry? The spiritual guidance that is probably most helpful is found in the fourth chapter of Philippians, where the Apostle Paul is writing to the worried Philippians: "Rejoice in the Lord alway, and again I say, Rejoice." There is a place where we have to make up our minds to follow this God-given advice.

In this chapter, we shall dwell upon three areas in which we must take the initiative and make up our minds to do the things that will enable God to help us master worry.

I.

Make up your mind to be happy in Christ.

"Rejoice in the Lord alway, and again I say, Rejoice." It is reported that Abraham Lincoln said toward the end of his life: "I have been about as happy as I have made up by mind to be." That is it. Make up your mind to be happy, and quite likely you will experience happiness. That is literally following the counsel of the Apostle Paul in Scripture: "Rejoice in the Lord," or, "Be happy in the Lord."

We Americans claim to pity ignorant savages who live in terror of their cruel gods and their demons who keep their minds in slavery. However, when we worry, are we not ourselves slaves of a demon which terrorizes our hopes and casts its cruel shadow across all of life? We must determine to make it our business to be happy in Christ. Robert Louis Stevenson used to say: "This my task, happiness." Both he and Abraham Lincoln had terrific conflicts to face. Both men died early. Both men bore intolerable burdens. But both men impressed other people with a basic happiness of life in spite of their problems.

Do we, as Christians, impress people that way, or have we become professional mourners? Do we have something of the true gladness of God printed upon us? We can have it if we will make up our minds to let God give it to us. In life, like in a painting, it is possible to look upon the shadows more than the light. Why not make up your mind to let the portrait of your life have that famous Rembrandt lighting, then look upon the gold, the light, and the flesh tints rather than those darkening browns.

Remember, God wants you to be a happy person in Christ. That does not mean you are going to be happy in yourself, nor does it mean that you will always be happy with other people and circumstances. It shall be as Paul states: "Be happy in Christ." Because He has come to bring us happiness, because He is the incarnate Son of God, because He said: "I have come that ye may have life and have it more abundantly," and because He holds the whole world in His hands. "Rejoice in the Lord, alway, and again I say, Rejoice." Make up your mind to be happy in Christ.

II.

Make up your mind not to worry. This may be easier said than done, but it can be accomplished. The one lady made up her mind to budget her worries. Another made up her mind to turn her worries over to God. Both worked. We make up our mind to do a lot of other things. We make up our minds to get up earlier in the morning, and certainly this is easier said than done, but we do it. We make up our minds to clean the garage, we make up our minds to study, and we make up our minds to keep that appointment, etc. Then, surely, we can make up our minds to be "Careful for nothing," as the Apostle Paul further states it. Do not spend the good energy that it takes to be worrisome about something. Simply make up your mind not to worry.

One way to make up your mind not to worry is to let your mind remember that most of the worries you have will never come true. We approach a thousand and one rivers with the thought there will be no bridge there, but only one time in a thousand do we ever find it missing. We invent imaginary difficulties to worry about. We fear the worst, but it seldom happens. Most of our worrisome premonitions are as unreal as the ghosts in the cemetery. It is foolish to borrow trouble and worry out of nowhere. I, along with just about everyone else, have often feared the worst, thinking some terrible evil was going to come about but it hardly ever does. Ninety per cent of the things I have worried about never come to pass. For half of the 10 per cent that did come to pass, I have been able to get expert help to enable me to handle them. If I have a medical problem, I see my doctor; if I have a legal problem, I see my attorney; if I have a financial problem, I see my banker. With the remaining problems, God has been able to help me through when I have been willing to listen to Him and follow His guidance. Why should I worry about these things when I have help like that?

It is also well to remember that these worries which loom so large now will not seem so large "a twelfth month and a day from now," as Samuel Johnson says in Boswell's biography of him. You can make up your mind to be happy and to have your life so filled with good things that there will not be any time for this fretting worry.

"People ask me daily," said a lady, "when they look at my face without a wrinkle, what I do to keep so young. I tell them that whenever I felt a wrinkle coming I have smiled it away and refuse to worry about it."

Make up your mind to smile, to be happy in Christ, and not to worry.

III.

Make up your mind to be happy. The truly thankful person seldom worries. Life is too rich and good for him to be cluttered up with much worry. The Apostle Paul follows his famous counsel of: "Rejoice in the Lord," just two verses later by saying that we should do these things "with thanksgiving" (Philippians 4:6). As we live the happy, joyful worry-free life with thanksgiving, we do not mean thanksgiving in a general and diffused way.

This thankful life we are calling to help master worry is not a thanks that says, "I am thankful for everything and for a good life." That is too general. We are thinking about being thankful in a particular way so that we can sit down and write it out specifically. One person might write: "I am thankful that God has given me at least a certain degree of health of mind and body. I thank God for friends, those who help me with the problems of life. I thank Him for the ability to see, to hear, and the opportunity to move about in my community and world. I thank God for the ability to be sensitive to His divine will and His uplifting challenge." You may build your list, writing down the things for which you are thankful, and I promise you it will work wonders, helping you to master worry.

We believe in a God who is in control of this universe, this world in which we live, and He is a God who will never turn pale. Trust Him, and do not worry. Be of good cheer. "Rejoice in the Lord alway, and again I say, Rejoice." Make up your mind to do the things He would have you do, and joy, happiness and peace will be yours.

PRAYER: Our Heavenly Father, grant unto us this day and every day the ability to make up our mind to perform and practice what Thou hast through Thy Holy Word proclaimed and through Thy Holy Spirit been given the power to do. Amen.

18. HOW TO BUILD CHARACTER

"Let this mind be in you, which was also in Christ Jesus"
(Philippians 2:5).

CHARACTER IS WHAT YOU REALLY ARE. IT IS NOT WHAT you think you are. We can be deceived at this point. Character is not what your wife or husband thinks you are. (You may wish it were, or you may be glad it is not!) Character is not what your friends think you are, and certainly not what your enemies think you are. Character is your real genuine self. It is what God knows you are. A good character is one of the finest assets a person can have for the obtaining of and living the good life.

Thus, is it not strange that many a young man or woman will spend hours training to excel in sports, music, and charm, and yet be unwilling to submit to the disciplines for the building of good character and integrity? Moreover, is it not even more strange that many parents fail to lead their children into the paths of character-building disciplines and adventures because they are so busy developing the muscle of money-making, or specializing at the club, or have succumbed to the idea that all training of the children can be left to the school and the church?

The fallacy of leaving such training to the school and church is that we forget that we are the school and the church; that they are what we are. If we are not a part of these institutions with our interest and our prayers, they are not complete and cannot properly train our children in character building. We need to be a part of the character-building organizations if the work is to be properly done. The school, the church, the club, the society, and organizations, such as scouts, all make their impression upon the budding character of every young person exposed to them.

Parents need to stand with their children in all of these areas of life, and share with them the pain of young defeat, which will surely come at times; and, then they will have the opportunity to share with them the thrill of youthful victory. You do that, then some day you will have the supreme thrill of seeing him stand alone against the world, strong in character.

Ever make the mistake of thinking that good character can come without some diligent training, effort, and hard work? Your finest character building organizations and enterprises, such as church, youth groups, boys clubs, scouts, all require a lot of good hard work. You cannot just say: "I will send my children to Sunday school, or to a scout troop, and see what they can do for them." We all need to get into the act, serve on the committees and support the efforts with all our strength if we are going to build character in our boys and girls.

Most adults can use some building of character themselves, and a person can build in himself character in no finer way than by seeking to help others. It is as Herbert Spencer once said: "By no political alchemy can we get golden conduct out of leaden instincts. But instincts can be changed; fresh grafts can be introduced upon the stock; the whole tree can be trained in a new direction, and so golden conduct be made to flow from a golden character."

Let us now survey three attributes, the developing of which will make for a fine, upright, noble Christian character: conscience, love and will power.

I.

First of all, develop a well-trained conscience.

Conscience is that ability of the soul or mind to distinguish between right and wrong. Just as it is easier to train the tender shoot early as it comes up through the soil to grow in the right direction, so it is easier to train the conscience when one is young. However, it is never too late to turn to God and His program of righteousness. Also, it is very important to train the conscience to be in harmony with God's will and laws. If our conscience is not trained, and we do not know right from wrong, we will perhaps do wrong ignorantly. However, it is still wrong, and we will have to suffer the consequences. Also we will suffer the sting of bad character.

No one can do wrong and get by with it very long. No one can do wrong and have good character. Doing right has to start in the conscience—in the mind. "Let this mind be in you which was in Christ Jesus." Think the thoughts of Christ after Him. Study His teachings. Memorize His sayings. Many criminals have confessed that before they committed their first crime, they had performed it many times in their minds. On the other hand, the one who rises to great heights of character and goodness will have had his mind dwelling upon the good things of God, building within himself a good, well-trained conscience.

A certain speaker was lecturing to a group of junior high young people on the subject of conscience. He endeavored to illustrate his subject by telling how he went hunting with his bird dog. The dog ran here and there through the brush and finally stopped. With one foot lifted, he looked with intensity right at a certain spot. They went toward the spot, and soon a covey of quail flew up. The hunter shot and got his quail.

The speaker then asked the question: "How did the dog know those quail were there?" He started to answer his own question, when a small boy shouted: "The dog had brains." When the students became quiet, he explained that they all had brains but would not have known the quail were there.

He then went on to say that it took more than brains to sense the presence of quail. God gave the dog a special instinct that, when trained properly, could point out to a hunter just where the quail were located. Likewise, God has given to us, His children, an instinct called conscience that will help us to tell the difference between right and wrong when it is trained in the ways of the Lord.

First of all develop your conscience by studying the life and teachings of Christ, letting His mind speak to your mind. "Let this mind be in you, which was also in Christ Jesus."

II.

We build character by what we love. The things we love are the things that soon become a part of us.

First of all, one will want to love God. We have a verse of Scripture that says: "We love him, because he first loved us" (I John 4:19). Sometimes, we may doubt the love of God. We may doubt the love of other people when they do truly love us. This is due to our own weakness and does not cancel the fact of love. It cancels only our keen awareness of it. Sharpen up your awareness of God's love for you, and then love God as the Scripture commands, "with all your heart, soul and strength." We can do this by engaging in hours of prayer, worship, and the total fellowship the church provides.

This leads us to state that we ought also to love the church; love to go to church; love to be a part of it.

Then, of course, a proper love for God and His church will lead us to love one another. The Apostle Paul saw how many persons were seething with hostility and resentment toward another, and so he issued a call to love: "Let all bitterness, and wrath, and anger, and clamour, and evil speaking be put away from you, with all malice: and be kind one to another, tenderhearted, forgiving one another, even as God for Christ's sake hath forgiven you" (Ephesians 4:31, 32).

God's purpose for Christians is that they love one another. Without love, friction can be created among God's children because of personal ambition, human weakness, division of opinion, lack of understanding, and general irritation because of a difference of personality and temperament. It also means that we are to love those who curse us, do good to those who hate, and pray for those who despitefully use us and persecute us. Why? "That ye may be the children of your Father which is in heaven," and build strong, stalwart character. Again, "Let *this* mind be in you which was also in Christ Jesus"—the mind of love.

Develop a sensitive, trained, Christian conscience and then learn to love as Christ loved.

III.

Finally, that we may be able to put this training and love to work in life, develop a strong, vigorous will power.

The will needs also to be trained and made strong. A strong will power trained in the ways of righteousness and honesty will result in the getting of good things done in the world.

The story is told of a farm hand endeavoring to get a balking mule to move. A woman, watching from the road, said: "Are you going to let that mule get the best of you? Where is your will power?" The man replied: "My will power is right here, all right, but you ought to come out here and measure this mule's *won't* power." With all the negative won't power of evil in the world, the Christian, if he is to maintain a good character must develop a strong will power.

How to build good character? Develop a God-trained conscience, a love for the good things of God, and finally, let God build within you a strong will power. Good character, the good life, all things of good come from God. Take the word "good" and take away from it the letters G–O–D, and what do you have left? Only one little zero, a nothingness to build upon. We need God if we are to build good character. Let Him speak to you in Christ. Seek to be like Him in your tastes, your desires, and your actions.

A bee on the hillside flies down over the city, passes by all the garbage barrels, all the dirt and ugliness of the city streets, and finds a beautiful flower. He stops, gets his honey, and makes a beeline back to his home on the hillside. Why does he do this? Because he is a bee.

A buzzard swoops down the hillside. He flies over the city, passes all the flowers and beautiful things, until he finds the carcass of a dead animal. Flying around a bit as though he were looking to see if anyone were watching, he sweeps down and grabs the dead animal, and away he goes with it. Why did he do that? Because he was a buzzard.

Our children grow up, become young people, then young adults. They go away to college, go to work, or take a position in the city. In a short while they will disclose whether they are bees or buzzards. Their character, good or bad, will show.

Those who love moral carrion, who want to get rich off the decay and death of our communities, and indulge in the gratification of personal desires, without consideration for moral law and practical results, are the buzzards. Those who love the sweet things, the fine things, the good things of life, letting a good character show, are the bees.

Develop a good character and become a bee, not a buzzard. Let me just summarize now in a couple of crude poetic lines:

> Has God deserted people,
> And left it up to you
> To do just as your passions please,
> And not care what you do?
> Oh, no, He's still in business,
> And knows what kind of road we plod;
> So when you're building character,
> Just remember, you need — God.

PRAYER: Gracious God, Thou who dost train our conscience, who has taught us to love in Christ, who dost give us power to live the life Thou hast given, we would come to Thee to seek and find good character, and lend our lives to the values that last forever and make us more worthy of the life eternal. Amen.

19. FROM WORMS TO ANGELS VIA HUMOR

"A merry heart doeth good like a medicine"   *(Proverbs 17:22).*

TOO MANY OF US ARE SIMPLY WORKING TOO HARD AND ARE too solemn for our own good. If only we could smile more it would aid us in good health and help to carry us through the storms of life.

When people are asked to list the traits they like to see in others, usually a sense of humor will appear high on that list. I met a man one evening who knew Winston Churchill, and he told a group of us some of the more intimate things concerning the Prime Minister. One of them was his sense of humor as it was revealed more privately. He told of what happened just after Churchill had finished that famous speech through which he pulled England together in her darkest hour. As you will recall, he said: "We will fight them on the land, we will fight them on the sea, and we will fight them in the air." Then, when he sat down, he whispered to the man next to him: "I should have told them we will hit them over the head with beer bottles, because that's just about all we have left." In our darkest hour we need our sense of humor.

I believe the really great men of the faith have seen this through the centuries. Here are some thoughts from a Congregational pastor of the past century, George B. Cheever, who said: "Health is the constant enjoyment of life; give me a keen and ever present sense of humor . . . . it is the next best thing to an abiding faith."

I do believe most ministers have learned quite well to laugh with one another. We deal with serious subjects so much that we are very much in need of good humor once in a while. What I am saying is that it is spiritually good for us to laugh at ourselves and to laugh with one another. We should not laugh at people, but rather laugh with them.

I.

One of the basic spiritual needs of mankind is a simple understanding of himself.

When we are able to see ourselves as others do, we are surprised at all the laughs that are in store for us. Too many pretend to be something or somebody they are not. My, how we put on. We need something that will bring us down off these pedestals on which we place ourselves, pedestals of importance, intellectualism, prideful piety, self-pity, touchy tempers. If we could only come down, my, what a laugh we would have. This laughter would have a healthy effect, too.

We do not get off these pedestals with a false humility, either. False humility still keeps the joke on us. For example: if I should preach an average sermon some Sunday, and someone would say to me: "You had a good sermon today," and I would reply: "Oh, it was really nothing. I spent only two or three hours on it," I would, in effect, be assuming a posture of false humility, and be really saying between the lines: "If you thought this was good, just think how good it would have been if I had spent ten hours on it."

Then there is the lady who is always saying "My, but my hair looks terrible. I just can't keep it looking nice." All the time that she is saying it, she really thinks it looks the best of all in the room and is just hinting for someone to say it. One time when a lady did this, a rather bold fellow said to her. "Yes, I believe you are right. Your hair does look terrible." You never saw a woman more angry in all your life. It's a real sense of honest humility that brings us down off these pedestals, and good humor will help do it.

II.

Not only does good humor give us a better understanding of ourselves, it is scientifically established that it is one of our best medicines.

How true are the words of Scripture: "A merry heart doeth good like a medicine." This verse is good medical advice today, but was written over 2000 years ago, and it had probably been in the oral teachings centuries before that. One hymn writer has put it this way: "I will laugh and love and lift." A psychologist has said: "The more you laugh, the longer you laugh, and the easier you laugh, the *healthier* is your personality." He then goes on to say: "The neurotic who can laugh at himself is on the road to cure."

Everyone was simply amazed at the health and vigor and sweet disposition of a certain ninety-four-year-old man. How could this be, considering the fact that he had been married for seventy years to a woman noted for her temper? "Well, it was this way," he said. "When she and I were married, we agreed that whenever either one of us would become angry, I would go out for a walk, and I have been living an outdoor life ever since." My, how a bit of humor can change the most difficult situation. Humor will not only make us easier to live with, but will actually make us healthier.

Of course, our concern for personal health is not the only thing in which we are interested, and it is not an end in itself, but this area of life and spiritual make-up are closely related. We are interested in a well rounded understanding of the integration of all the life: physical, mental, and spiritual.

Thus, I'm maintaining that when one sees his faith in its full scope of life, he finds that humor is not anti, or irreligious, but truly a God-given faculty which contributes to health, and to spiritual and religious maturity.

"Good humor," said the Earl of Shaftsbury, "is the clear blue sky to the soul." Notice that he said: "Good humor." We must place the emphasis on *good*. There is a lot said and done that brings a laugh which is not necessarily good humor. Too much religious emphasis of the past has been done with a false identification of the religious with the somber, long-faced, imposed pious look. Oh, the damage it has done! In one church someone commented on how solemn and mournful the people looked as they were singing . . . . : "Joyful, Joyful. We adore Thee."

I really believe we can be pleasantly reverent and worshipful, that we can be warmly and joyously alert to the precious and wonderful promises of God. Good humor and the pleasantness which it helps to bring to the personality is a gift of God adding to that deep and wonderful glow which will be contagious in helping to bring peace and health to others.

III.

Finally, we must show joy on the outside if people are to believe we have it within.

We can talk all day, but we will never convince many that we have the joy of God's presence inside when we look so mournfully downhearted on the outside. If that's having the "Joy, Joy, Joy, Joy, Down in Our Hearts," people will not want it. I'm really afraid the wrong identification has been made with religion, even to the extent of dress. One time, as a theological student, I went to a clothing store and inquired about a black suit. The salesman said: "I don't think you want a black suit. The only ones who wear black are ministers and funeral directors." I finally got a black suit and many are the times when I have been wearing it, some stranger has said to me, after we were engaged in conversation: "I knew you were a minister. You just looked like one."

On the other hand, one day, when I was wearing my black suit, I just slipped off my coat and put on a sport coat that blended with the black trousers. I also had on a black tie with a little bright red in it that matched the red handkerchief in the pocket of my sport coat. I stopped at the hotel coffee shop, and while there got to talking to a young medical student. We discussed world problems and a few social subjects. Then he asked: "By the way, what do you do?" I said: "I'm a minister." He looked at me, and said: "Well, you sure don't look like it." I asked: "Why?" He said: "I guess it is the way you are dressed."

I suppose he expected a minister to be someone old, in all dark clothes, with the frown of a stoic. Somewhere there has been too much unhealthy, long-faced approach to Christianity.

When I make my calls, going to the homes and hospitals, I see no reason why I cannot wear a bright red tie, a glowing yellow one, or a pleasing blue if I desire. The flowers we take to the hospital rooms — from God's creation—are of these cheerful hues, so why cannot God and the church be represented attractively and cheerfully?

The story is told of a visiting preacher who one morning dragged himself into the pulpit looking sad and discouraged. His sermon was sad and gloomy, and he began his prayer with some of the thoughts of man from the Old Testament, calling himself and the congregation: "Poor worms of the dust." A certain wise and godly woman in the congregation that morning told her husband: "That man needs a good meal and a good time today. Let's invite him home for dinner." He was invited to the fine, joyful Christian home.

That evening when he went to the service he stepped to the pulpit like a mighty conqueror. He began his evening prayer by saying: "Thank you, God, that you have created us 'just a little lower than the angels.'" That is it. Not only can a good meal lift us from "worms in the dust" to "a little lower than the angels," so can humor.

There is a lot of humor in the Bible. Much of it is implied, not direct. Consider the time Jesus told the Pharisees: ". . . you see the speck that is in your brother's eye, but do not notice the log that is in your own eye" (Matthew 7:3 RSV). My, how the common people must have laughed when they heard the way the Pharisee was tumbled from his pedestal.

Consider how little children flocked around Jesus. Do children flock around a gloomy-looking stranger? Rarely! Jesus simply had to have the warm smile, the cheerful attitude, and, at times, a laughing humor, or children would not have been so eager to be with Him. Cheerfulness and a bit of humor with wisdom and understanding is unbeatable.

Just because one does not conduct his affairs, preach and practice his Christian Faith with a long, somber face does not mean it is not serious and meaningful. In fact, it is often more meaningful to the genuine humorist than the long-faced person who is only putting up a pious front.

"A merry heart doeth good like a medicine." A deep reverence for all of life, a love for people and eternal things, crowned with a real and rich sense of humor, can lift us from "worms in the dust" to "a little lower than the angels." And we need lifting up. Oh, how we need it.

We know there are many things wrong in this world. We feel beaten down much of the time and much of what we see is heartbreaking. There is a breakdown of honesty and integrity, escape to alcohol, sickness of various kinds, personal storms within one's soul at times, discouragement and possibility of war, etc. In the midst of it all, we need lifting up. Even in the stormy, dark hours, we dare not lose our sense of humor, for humor can help us get our feet out of the mire. Most certainly we will have a better understanding of ourselves. We will be more healthy. We will have a greater spiritual maturity, and God shall be truly glorified in all that we do.

In short, we will be able to sing a new song and more effectively witness to the inner joy that God can give. We shall be able, not only to know personally the good life, but also really share the "Good News" that others may know the good life and help all of us to stay alive as long as we live.

PRAYER: Almighty God, Father of all joy and beauty, may there be cultivated in us a reverence for truth and beauty and goodness. Grant unto us an understanding of ourselves and others, that we may be able to develop this proper expression and spirit for the sharing of the "Good News" that there may be healing, salvation, joy, and peace on earth, good will toward men. Amen.

20. BEAUTY IS MORE THAN SKIN DEEP

"Let the beauty of the Lord our God be upon us"   *(Psalm 90:17).*

A LADY RECENTLY WROTE: "MY BEAUTY IS GONE, MY young friends are few, and I am lonely. How can I make new friends when I am no longer attractive?"

This question reveals a wrong understanding of real beauty. It assumes the old, erroneous saying that "Beauty is only skin deep." This is a confusion of beauty with personality. It is true that there are some people, men and women, who have a facial surface, physical beauty that attracts at first glance. Such persons can quickly make friends without being gracious, warm, and friendly toward others. However, as the lady referred to above found, such friendships last only while the youthful beauty lasts.

If one is to have true, genuine, and lasting beauty that attracts and holds friends, he will have to have a beauty of personality that goes more than skin deep. There is no better way to have this than to follow the counsel of the psalmist, in Psalm 90, verse 17: "Let the beauty of the Lord our God be upon us."

Some time ago, while waiting in a barber shop, I noticed an article rather hurriedly and did not think too much about it at the time. It was a result of a question put to several prominent men in various fields of work. It was this: "What do you first notice in a woman?" Several weeks later, I noticed in the fine writer, Sidney Harris' column, that he, too, had read it and summarized what he considered to be some important items. He noted that some of the answers were, of course, suggestively facetious, and others were solemn, but that the only reply that showed any real insight was made by Oleg Cassini, the dress designer.

. He notes that Mr. Cassini did not mention the figure, the posture, the clothes, nor any other superficial aspect that might be expected from one connected with costuming. He said, rather: "What I first notice is her mouth, then her eyes. Her mouth tells me how she feels about herself. Her eyes say how she feels about other

116

people, including me." This is getting at the real person, the personality from which comes real lasting beauty.

Is it not strange that many people, men and women, will spend hundreds of dollars each year to improve their looks, and this is proper when done in moderation and good taste, but if the mouth is resentful and discontented, if the eyes are greedy and calculating, all of this vast expenditure will have been tossed down the drain. Beauty is more than skin deep. It is not a matter of looks alone. Real, true, lasting beauty comes when we "Let the beauty of the Lord our God be upon us." How do we let the beauty of the Lord come upon us? This is what we want to now consider.

I.

"Worship the Lord in the beauty of holiness."

This phrase is used three times in the Old Testament (I Chronicles 16:29; Psalms 29:2, 96:9). We read in the book of Genesis that it was God who made the world and called it good—beautiful. Also, the text we have frequently referred to in these chapters begins with these words: "Whatsoever things are lovely"—beautiful in personality—"think on these things."

If you want to think beautiful thoughts, grow beautiful in personality, and share beauty with others, then Worship the Lord in "sacred vestments" (Moffatt). What does this symbolic language mean? I think it means this: Do not come to worship in garments of egotism, pride and self-righteousness. Do not come to worship in judges' robes and sit in stern judgment upon the pastor, the choir, and the one sitting next to you, in front of you, or across the aisle from you. Come with the mind and soul clothed in the garments of humility before the Lord. When a person has this attitude he can rise and go out into the world with the thoughts of God and the imprint of God upon him. "Whatsoever things are lovely, think on these things."

After having worshiped God in the "beauty of holiness," man can go forth with thoughts of beauty, which he got from God who created all things beautiful.

II.

Realize and know that the highest beauty—beauty far superior to facial and features—is within the reach of everybody.

If you long for beautiful personality, beautiful character, claim it as your birthright, given by God, stick to it with all possible tenacity, and you will not only prepare yourself to receive it, but will also increase your power to attract it.

The basis of all real beauty is a kindly, godly, helpful heart, and a desire to share the beauty of good cheer and sunshine everywhere, and this, shining through the face, even makes it appear more beautiful. John Ruskin said: "Every right action and true thought sets the seal of its beauty on person and face." If one will hold the beauty thought: "Whatsoever things are lovely," persistently in the mind, he will leave such an impression of beauty, sweetness and harmony wherever he goes that it will rise above and outshine any plainness, or uncomeliness.

Too many people dwell upon what they think of their unfortunate plainness, or lack of beauty so long that they exaggerate it. Actually, they are not nearly so plain nor devoid of beauty as they think they are, and were it not for the fact that they have made themselves so sensitive and self-conscious about it, others would not notice it at all.

Jesus has cautioned us about too much emphasis on surface or artificial beauty, and calls our attention to the beauty of God. Hear Him in the Sermon on the Mount: "Consider the lilies of the field, how they grow; they toil not, neither do they spin: and yet I say unto you, That even Solomon in all his glory was not arrayed like one of these" (Matthew 6:28, 29).

God, who has created the lilies of the field in all their beauty, has also created His children to be beautiful in His image, that is, in personality, in character, and in spirit. Then that beauty will shine through the face, making it more beautiful. "Let the beauty of the Lord our God be upon us."

III.

We now call to your attention several examples of how this emerging beauty can become a reality.

Abraham Lincoln was not, by most people, considered to be a handsome man. In fact, a lot has been said about his awkwardness and ugliness. Yet, on the other hand, because of his compassion, a depth of kindliness in his eyes, and an expression of sincerity in his face, Abraham Lincoln was considered one of the loveliest of men.

I know two brothers, one of whom married a lady who was considered beautiful; the other married one whom most people would not call beautiful. The first one married the so-called beautiful lady twice, and she divorced him twice. The other man, talking to me about it one day, said this: "I did not get a beauty queen like my brother did, but I married a lady with a beautiful heart, and I still have her. My brother never had a wife with a beautiful heart, and now, he doesn't even have her face." He was so right. One lady talking to me about this lady with the beautiful heart said: "She is a diamond in the rough, and I dearly love her."

I recently heard of a very lovely woman who was described as having a face like a horse. It was long and lean; her eyes were widely spaced; her ears were large, and her front teeth were spaciously white and alarming. At first glance one thought unkindly of her. However, she was one of the most popular women among her fellowship. She was humorous, sympathetic, unselfish, and generous. Whenever anyone was in need, she was there to give aid and assistance. She lived to be nearly ninety, and her funeral was the largest ever held in her town. One time, commenting on her looks, she offered this testimony: "If I had been a beauty, I would not have made the effort to make friends, and now I have to thank my plain face for the years of happiness my friendships have brought me."

I think all of us have known people like that. What a contrast they are to the ones with lots of physical beauty, yet revealing through the bitter mouth and the tortured eyes a basic dissatisfaction with themselves and the world around them.

There are men and women who have both a lot of natural beauty and a beauty of personality. It is wonderful to have both, but not many do.

I am thinking of two men of my intimate acquaintance. One of them is a dashing, handsome man, a good talker who makes friends with speed, influences people briefly. However, with equal speed, people see through him and the popularity of this handsome man quickly fades. The other man was a professor I had in New York City. At first, a person was not attracted toward him at all. However, as one got to know him, one found a beautiful heart, a strong personality, a Christ-like spirit. Early in my experience with his class, one of the students said to me: "This professor grows on you." He was right. He was so beautiful in his spirit and outlook on life; the longer you knew him, the more that first impression, that physical impression, faded from view, and one saw the spirit of Christ shine through clearly and radiantly.

If you are what people consider naturally beautiful, well and good. This is fine. However, regardless of your physical looks, the real beauty that is deep and lasting comes when we "Let the beauty of the Lord our God be upon us." How do we do this? "Worship the Lord in the beauty of holiness." Realize that this God-given beauty is within your reach. Think of all the people who have given themselves to God who have found this beauty and are graciously sharing it with others.

> Let the beauty of Jesus be seen in me,
> All His wonderful passion and purity;
> O Thou Spirit Divine, all my nature refine,
> Till the beauty of Jesus is seen in me.
>
> —Albert Osborne

PRAYER: Almighty God, save us from a way of life that would place too limited a view upon what is really beautiful, and teach us to cherish the beauty of godly character, the graciousness of personality, and the sharing of the beauty of holiness with others, making life really worth-while. Amen.

21. THERE IS NO WRONG SIDE OF SIXTY

"Teach us to number our days that we may get a heart of wisdom"
(Psalm 90:12, RSV).

A FEW MONTHS AGO I HEARD A WOMAN REPLY, WHEN someone asked her age: "Well, I have to admit that I am on the wrong side of sixty."

Of course, what she meant was that she was over sixty years of age. However, I would like to state that there is no wrong side of sixty. I firmly believe that any age is good and right for us at the time. If it is a disaster to grow old, then we must logically conclude that it was a disaster to have been born. Everyone who is born begins that moment to grow older. The only way not to grow old is to die early. This pathway upward into greater age is God's will for us, and all along the way His love and wisdom are expressed. He has asked us to all along the way to number our days that we may get a heart of wisdom. Each advancing age teaches us something more, and we should accept all this graciously and with joy.

Thus, let us not be fretful, irritable and touchy about the process of aging, and in complete, utter dejection wish we could evade the natural order of things. No properly thinking person in his better moments, if he were given his choice, would even accept this life in the world except on the conditions of aging and the coming change which we call death, whereby we enter into eternal life.

Is it not strange how we so often become sensitive about our age and want to hide it. I heard of a fellow who had just found a new lady friend and someone asked him how old she was. He replied: "She says she has lived thirty-two summers, but I heard afterward that she has spent most of her life at the North Pole."

A man applying for a job was told: "We did have a vacancy, but you are too late," and this man, sensitive about his age, said: "Yeah, about ten years too late."

I read the other day, however, about a situation that turned out quite differently. A man found it necessary to employ a new secretary. Three applicants fully met the requirements for the job. He hired the attractive blond, but she did not show up for work. Next he hired the young brunette, who was also very pretty. She lasted only a week. The man mentioned to his wife that the third candidate was really too old—fifty-five—so he would have to rule her out. His wife replied indignantly: "Well, I am fifty-five. Am I too old to do the work you expect of me?" The account concludes that Bill believes his new secretary, age fifty-five, is the best and most efficient he has ever had. Age need not take away the good life, ambition, productivity, happiness, joy, or love.

> Age is a quality of mind.
> If you have left your dreams behind,
> If hope is lost,
> If you no longer look ahead,
> If your amibtions' fires are dead,
> Then you are old.

> But if from life you take the best,
> And if in life you keep the jest,
> If love you hold,
> No matter how the years go by,
> No matter how the birthdays fly,
> You are not old!
> —Author Unknown

In this chapter I am seeking to discuss how we should approach this matter of aging that we may gain a heart of wisdom.

I.

It is good for us to remember that every age is good and has its rewards.

It seems that children and young people want to be older. It is difficult for them to realize that their age is good for them. I can remember hearing students of college age longing to be a bit older, mostly so that they would be earning money. They would sometimes say something like this: "When I get out into life." They forgot that they were in life right then, living it with all its opportunities for them at their age. Most people do not take proper advantage of those early years and all of the opportunities they afford for the getting of a heart of wisdom.

However, greater fear and anxiety comes as a result of growing older and wishing we were younger. Worshiping at the shrine of youth seems to be an American psychosis. Many people are simply horrified at the thought of leaving their twenties behind. Yet a person will have wonderful experiences in his thirties, and ones that will add to his heart of wisdom, ones that he could not have possibly had in his twenties. Then when it comes to moving from the thirties to the forties, many are just simply panic-stricken. Like the famous comedian, they simply get stuck at thirty-nine, and there they stay for ten or twenty years. Now this age is really not so bad, and we need to accept that as a truth. In fact, someone said: "A woman's best ten years are between thirty-nine and forty."

While we may joke about growing older, the really mature person does not worry and fret about it one bit. Actually, the mature, well-adjusted person wants to be exactly the age that he is, because this is the context in which God has placed him, and it is right for him. One man, commenting along this line, said: "I am grateful for the years when I was young, but I am content to leave them in memory. I have no wish to live them again." As a mature Christian gentleman, he was happy to be the age he was. He found his age to be good.

As we have stated, every age is good. However, there are so many ways in which forty can be better than twenty. At forty you can be more what you want to be than at twenty. At forty, fifty, and sixty, we become more what we have made ourselves. Perhaps one of the fears of growing older is the added responsibility the years bring. The older we are, the more responsible we are for what we are. Real mature achievement that brings happiness is to make the best of your every age as you live it. Mature men and women wish to be exactly the age they are, because that age is good and proper for them. Such maturity will make the best use of every age for the obtaining of a greater heart of wisdom.

II.

Also, we all should seek to grow old gracefully. When one grows old gracefully, he somehow, in the light of maturity, comes to feel that this is the best age of all, and the pleasures of youth seem less attractive than the satisfactions of later life. Someone has said: "One of the compensations of old age is that you do not have to pretend to be dignified to impress the old folks." Truly, the compensations are there in every age.

However, there are many who cannot seem to grow old gracefully. They become sensitive and bitter about it. I heard about an elderly lady who lived next door to the minister, and she became ill. The minister, being new in the community, wanted to know how old she was, that he might find someone her age to go and be with her. To show his friendly interest, he sent his young son over to find out how old Mrs. Johnson was. The boy went and came back quickly, saying: "Mrs. Johnson says that it is none of your business how old she is."

Sad to say, the years do leave many bitter, without having gained the heart of wisdom that makes us grateful for our friends, the love of God and life itself. Like the Bourbon kings, they have learned nothing from the flow of years, and have forgotten nothing, clinging tenaciously to the prejudice and ideas and opinions they had in childhood and adolescence. One's idea of God in childhood may remain his idea of God in middle age, if he is not continually gaining a heart of wisdom. His egotism of sixteen may turn into the stubbornness of sixty. The tantrums of childhood may become the emotional explosions of middle age. One may move up through the years and gain everything except wisdom. When this happens to a person, there is little wonder that he should grow old bitterly.

The real trick to growing old graciously is to stay alive as long as you live. Many do not do this. One pastor, having trouble with his deacons, penned this little poem and dedicated it to them:

Tell my deacons, when I am dead, to shed no tears,
For I will be no deader than they have been for years.

Stay alive as long as you live, keep an open mind, be willing to learn and accept new thoughts, and in the numbering of these days, continue to get a heart of wisdom.

Some do grow old gracefully, while some try to kid themselves into thinking it will not come to them, and fight it all the way. Josephine Lowman calls our attention to a poem that speaks to this point, saying she will bet the woman who wrote it never sits around just to re-live old memories.

How do I know my youth is all spent?
Well, my get up and go has got up and went.
But in spite of it all I'm able to grin
When I think of where my get up has been.

Old age is golden so I've heard said,
But sometimes I wonder when I get into bed,
With my ear in a drawer and my teeth in a cup,
My eyes on the table until I wake up.

As sleep dims my eyes I say to myself,
Is there anything else I should lay on the shelf?
But I'm happy to say as I close the door,
My friends are the same, perhaps even more.

When I was young, my slippers were red,
I could kick my heels over my head.
When I grew older, my slippers were blue,
But I still could dance the whole night through.

Now I am old, my slippers are black.
I walk to the store and puff my way back.
The reason I know my youth is all spent,
Is my get up and go has got up and went.

But I don't mind when I think with a grin
Of all the grand places my get up has been,
And since I've retired from life's competition
My schedules all scheduled (with complete
  repetition).

I get up each morning and dust off my wits,
Pick up the paper and read the obits.
I see my name missing, I know I'm not dead,
So I eat a good breakfast and go back to bed.

—Author Unknown.

The woman who wrote the above is growing old graciously, and shows no signs of bitterness, and probably will never become bitter, but continue gracious no matter how long she lives, and, as Miss Lowman stated: "May she live forever to add such vibrancy and humor to the troubled world."

III.

Place your faith in the assurance that old age in this life is the immediate prelude to eternal life with God.

In the numbering of our days, it certainly is at the heart of Christian wisdom to relate them to eternity. It certainly is not logical nor a part of wisdom to believe that the human spirit which can study the indestructibility of matter would itself be destructive. Certainly when we gain a true heart of wisdom, we come to know that the mind and spirit of man which can shape eternal ideas is just as eternal. It simply is not in the interest of wisdom to say that after one has matured and comes to the time of death, this ends all. There is too much evidence to the contrary.

Of course, it would be presumptuous of any of us to try to say with finality just what heaven is like, but we, as Christians, do firmly believe that old age is an immediate prelude to an eternal life in heaven with God. Also, in the New Testament, we find just a lifting of the curtain that we might catch a glimpse of the hereafter. John, describing his glorious vision of the heavenly realm, spoke symbolically of the hereafter in the grandest, most golden terms at his command. However, when he soared to the full weight of his majestic theme, he discarded all the trappings of symbolic language and abandoned all comparisons with the gold and pearls of this world, and begins to speak in purely spiritual language, saying: "The city had no need of the sun, neither of the moon, to shine in it: for the glory of God did lighten it, and the Lamb is the light thereof" (Revelation 21:23). "And God shall wipe away all tears from their eyes; and there shall be no more death, neither sorrow, nor crying, neither shall there be any more pain: for the former things are passed away" (Revelation 21:4). These are the fruits of maturity, of gaining the heart of wisdom, and growing old in Christ. Growing old is life—eternal life.

How should we grow old? First of all, remember that every age is good and has its rewards. Secondly, grow old gracefully with a spirit of love and good will toward all. Finally, place your faith in the assurance that old age is a prelude to something far better—eternal life with God and loved ones we have known. We all pass this way. God has planned it so. Let each step into age be with Him. Take Christ as your companion on this everlasting road.

> Oh, Comrades, moving onward toward the west,
> Whate'er our God decrees is best,
> And he who trusts in Him is blest.
>
> What though our day is growing old?
> The sky is flushed with sunset gold,
> And stars are issuing from their fold.
>
> What though the blackbird's flutings fail?
> We hear the plaintive nightingale
> Pour witching music through the vale.
>
> What though dear faces smile no more,
> Which were our joy in days of yore?
> They watch for us on yonder shore.
>
> Why should we fear the path to tread,
> Which all the myriads of the dead
> Have traversed under Christ, their head?
>
> Kings, sages, priests have passed this way,
> And freed from weakness and decay,
> Moved on into the light of day, —

The light eternal that fades no more
Glowing on that celestial shore
Where seraphim and saints adore.

— R.P.D.

Walking close to God, hand in hand with Christ, as one moves into age and maturity, the closer he comes to the sunset of earth, the closer is the sunrise of heaven.

PRAYER: We thank Thee Lord that Thou hast made all days good. Help us to move through them graciously with love in our hearts toward Thee and one another, and through faith in Thee become more worthy to dwell with Thee forever. Amen.

22. ASK GOD TO HELP YOU

*"Whatsoever ye shall ask in my name, that will I do, that the
Father may be glorified in the Son"*   *(John 14:13).*

MANY YOUNG PERSONS, AND YOUNG COUPLES JUST MARRIED,
starting life together, trying to establish and keep their home in-
tact on a modest budget, often take comfort in the belief that the
first years are the most difficult. They reason that, as time goes on,
there will be more money and that will take care of everything.
This is a mistake. Money, alone, will not make life any easier. It
will buy more things which we want, but it will not give one a
shining faith as a part of a living philosophy of life. It will not
change the temperament of certain difficult members of some
families.

Some people reason that education, alone, will unlock the door
to the good life. Certainly, education is necessary. The church has
always believed in education, having established the early univer-
sities, but the church has never said that education alone would
bring mankind to his salvation. There are today enough Ph.D.'s on
Skid Row or in prison to man a college. To live the good life and
carry into reality the high goals we have discussed in these chapters, we will, in the final analysis, have to ask God to help us.
Moreover, we will have to ask in the right way, with the right
spirit.

Catherine Marshall writes about a home that used to be filled
with tension because of an aunt's nagging faultfinding. The mother
prayed that God would take away the aunt's hypercritical attitude,
but nothing happened, except that the mother's resentment toward
the aunt increased. Catherine Marshall suggested that, instead of
just praying that the aunt would be changed, the mother should
pray for the well being of the whole family, and that they be
able to have fun and joy together. The mother then prayed something like this: "Lord, I know it is Your will that we have a happy
household. I ask that Your joy may flow full and free into our

home. Help us and auntie to have fun together and to find a new way of pleasing each other, and to rediscover laughter again."

A week later, the mother reported that things in the home were completely changed. Likewise, ask God to help you, but be sure to ask in the right spirit, the right way.

So often our turning to God is a crisis affair. There are thousands of people who pray only when they are under great stress, or strain, or in some danger. People who have never prayed before will pray when frightened, when the airplane engine gives out, when on a battlefield, when in a hospital, or when they approach any kind of danger, or death. If it is sincere, it is good to have these crises, catastrophic, driving, fire-engine prayers. That is what the psalmist had when he cried out: "O my Lord, God, hear my cry!" We need crisis prayer.

However, prayer, in its true sense, is not a futile cry of desperation born of fear or frustration. We need something more than crisis prayer. We need constant prayer. "Men ought always to pray, and not to faint" (Luke 18:1). This refers to the posture and position of the soul in relationship to God. When you pray, your physical posture is not nearly so important as the attitude of your heart. The astronauts speak of the attitude or position of the capsule as it speeds through orbit. Scott Carpenter and Gordon Cooper, because of the failure of the automatic control, had to give diligent attention to the manual operation of the attitude of the machine. The capsule had to have the right attitude toward the earth. Likewise, in prayer, we must have the right attitude toward God and others. This will not be automatic for us, either. We will have to give diligent attention toward the task of keeping in the right attitude and relationship to God. The hydrogen peroxide must be constantly working to keep the right attitude and proper orbit. We must have constant prayer for the culture of the worshiping soul and to keep the right attitude in the orbit of the love and will of God as we seek to wing our way through the atmosphere of the good life.

Prayer is also a controlling element in life. The Apostle Paul cried out: "The love of Christ controls us . . ." (II Corinthians 5:14, RSV). However, that controlling love is made operative through prayer. It is the dependable way to progress through life in the orbit of joy, cheerfulness, and goodness. It takes courage to do this for there are times when we are inclined to fall back into defeat and give up the fight. At times we want to retreat from the cutting edge of life, but it is out there in the rough of life where character is developed. It is there where we must turn to God and ask Him to help us to develop a cheerful personality and a stalwartness of character and integrity.

In the thirteenth and fourteenth chapters of John, we find a gloomy cloud hanging over the disciples of Jesus. They sensed the fact that something tragic was about to occur. They had been told, but they did not seem to realize just what was in the offing. One of them, the doubter, the questioner, Thomas, said: "We do not know where you are going; how can we know the way?" (John 14:5, RSV). The spirit of denial was already entering into Peter.

Judas had gone out into the darkest night of all history because he began to feel that this man, Jesus, would never really become king; so, with all his vast dreams of earthly empire shattered, he tried in the last minute, hasty decision to glean from this situation whatever he could. Thus, he went out and sold his Lord for thirty, dirty pieces of silver.

The dark cloud of gloom was hovering over James and John, also, for they were wrangling over their possible positions of power in the cabinet. In a mood like that, our Saviour humbly washed their feet in the ultimate of Christian service, teaching them the lesson that is at the heart of the Christian faith. In our arrogance, pride, and materialistic thinking, we need to ask the Saviour to help us, to teach us the lesson of humility, letting us know that we must depend on God.

With the gloomy cloud of the spirit filling the atmosphere, Jesus then gave to His disciples words which were like a beacon light on a dark starless night: "Let not your hearts be troubled: believe in God, believe also in me" (John 14:1, RSV). Jesus is the highest and the finest way to God. When we come to God by the way of Jesus Christ, we are coming by the way of the front door, and are quickly received into the throne room of God Himself. What an invitation to come to God by the way of Jesus Christ where we can ask Him to help us live the good life.

"Whatever you ask in my name, I will do it" (John 14:13, RSV), is the most dangerous text in the Bible if misinterpreted, but the most powerful text in all of God's Word, when rightly interpreted and applied in legitimate and holy ways.

In the remaining pages of this book, I want to discuss three ways we should pray and apply this verse to the living of the good life.

I.

Pray comprehensively. That means pray about everything. Do not be afraid to take everything to God in prayer. God is big enough for all your problems. Do not worry about any difficulty you may have in finding the right words and phrases as you pray about things. We are children of God, and we are learning and growing. He understands His children and wants us to come to Him with our needs, though we may be faltering in speech and expression.

When our three boys were learning to talk, they had difficulty in finding the right words, but they managed to make themselves understood to my wife and me. The mistakes they made only endeared them to us. When God sees His seeking growing children come to Him and endeavor to enter into prayer with Him about all things, even though we may be weak, stumbling and inadequate of speech, we will get through to God. Our sincere movement toward God will endear us to Him. In all your weakness, do not let anything remain outside the golden universe of prayer and God's complete interest in every detail of your life.

Not long ago a young man came to my study with a sordid story of life that most people would not want to tell to their doctor. He wondered if God would help him. Not long after that, another young man, thirty years old, was walking past the church very late at night and seeing a light in the window, came in, and asked: "I wonder if God would help me?" He was drunk and was running from the police. I told both men: "Of course, God will help you get straightened out if you really want Him to help, and if you sincerely ask Him to help you." I think the one man found real help when he asked God to help him. Concerning the other man, I do not know, for he is dead now because of the life he was living. No matter how great the problem, or how sordid the life, you can talk to God about it and ask Him for help.

The psychiatrist tells us that we have many fears which we harbor in our natures. In addition to those discussed in the earlier chapter, there are those about which we will want to talk to God if we are to really pray comprehensively. Many of us have a dreadful fear concerning our bodies. We are fearful that our organs will not function properly. Perhaps the heart will not keep up that steady beat with all the work it has to do. Maybe the lungs will fail to operate properly or the digestive system will fail to function correctly because we have swallowed something that failed to meet with a friendly reception committee upon its arrival in the stomach. Another troublesome fear about which others tell us is a fear of what our minds will do or fail to do. Will we be able to remember what we should remember? We sometimes fear that our sanity may be waning.

There is also a vast host of fears in connection with our emotional feelings. We are sometimes fearful of letting others see that we are emotionally touched. When Scott Carpenter's space capsule overshot some two hundred and fifty miles and there was much tension, concern, and anxiety in the voices of the reporters, I was so moved, so near to tears, that I went into the other room so that my wife and children would not see my emotion.

Another fear is that of doing something not socially acceptable, like wearing football shoes to a wedding or appearing at a party wearing a dress just like one on another woman. One time one of the men of the church and I appeared at the church wearing new suits which were exactly alike. It was quite by accident and we both remarked that, had we been women, neither of us would have worn the new suit again. Actually, there are many men and women who are dreadfully afraid they will not do things quite right, and in a way that is socially acceptable.

I list these fears, calling your attention to them, saying we should pray about all these things. Pray comprehensively. "Whatsoever ye shall ask in my name." Do not shut God out of any portion of your public or private life.

II.

Furthermore, let us pray conversationally. Prayer is not formal or a pious production in which you put a great deal of emphasis on the posture of your body or the position of the hands and then utter vain repetition of words that are proper for public and religious display. Prayer is a two-way conversation with God. So let us pray conversationally as we ask Him to help us live the life He has for us.

It is not necessary to assume any certain stance. I know there are some who feel they must kneel. Others feel that in order to pray in church they must stand. Still others feel that they must have certain things upon which to kneel. Some feel they must use a certain staid language, the language of the Elizabethan era of the King James version of the Bible. While kneeling is considered an act of humility when sincerely done, and while one's language should show a respect for God, none of this is so essential as entering into real conversation with the Father, with all of its give and take in both speaking and listening.

Some months ago, my family, a friend of the family, and myself were at the airport together one foggy night as a private plane was flying over our city, traveling from the West Coast to the East Coast. It was so foggy that the couple in the plane could not see the ground. They needed guidance, so they radioed the airport and asked for help. They spoke into the microphone and stated their needs. They then said "over" and turned the switch. They then listened to landing instructions. Conversation took place between the couple in the plane and the men at the airport. They expressed their need and got their answer. We soon saw them land as a result of that two-way conversation. Likewise, prayer, when we ask God for help, is a two-way conversation. Likewise, we must listen to His guidance. Prayer is, as Rosalind Rinker defined it in her book *Prayer—Conversing with God*, "a dialogue between two persons who love each other"—God and man. Prayer is a divine dialogue. Take all dullness and coldness out of your prayers and pray conversationally.

III.

Finally, pray conditionally. "Whatsoever you ask in my name." Never forget that prayer is to be "in His name." It is to be in His will. Even our Lord, in contrast to His own disposition at the moment, prayed: "O, my Father, if this cup may not pass away from me, except I drink it, thy will be done" (Matthew 26:42). Pray not to get just what you want, but pray also that you might be coupled with God's true purpose for you. This is the way to rise to the victories in life which we have been discussing in this book, and to achieve the good life.

We find the greatest happiness, not only in the blessings of God that come to our own personal lives, but also in the added blessing of being in line with God's divine plan for the world. The good life is found in the name of and in the will of God. Whenever we pray, we are to pray with that condition. At the bottom of all of God's prescriptions of all the spiritual illness and moral sickness of life must be the name of the Divine Physician.

A medical prescription is not valid unless a doctor has his signature at the bottom. I know that prescriptions, like prayers, at times are written in a mystical code that no one can read. But even though these prescriptions may appear to be surrounded by mystery, we know they are intricate and precise. There is in back of them the good mind and judgment of the doctor who diagnosed our need.

When we go to God in prayer, the solution to our problem, the meeting of our need must be in His name. Do not forget that your prayer is conditioned on God's superior knowledge of the total need, and He alone can be trusted to give the final approval to what we shall have and shall not have. Remember, pray "in His name."

I once heard a man tell how, as a boy in Texas, he wanted a new bicycle. Every night he would pray: "O God, give me this bicycle, the red one with the built-in tool chest, and with the special light and special siren." Yet, every morning, he would look under the bed and there would be no bicycle. Finally, God gave him the urge to go out and get a job to earn money to buy his bike. He got a job in the cotton fields, and all summer he cultivated cotton, and chopped cotton, and took cotton to the gin, until finally he was able to purchase his bicycle. That is the condition that we work and put ourselves into the finding of the answer. Pray conditionally.

Sometimes, throughout prayer, God transforms us. Recently, in a Bible conference, I heard and met a lady, who for years was an alcoholic. She has a son who, for many years, has been an alcoholic. He is no longer drinking, but has not yet come to know God. For years, she has been praying for that son and has asked thousands to pray for him. Though he has not yet come to God, her praying has transformed her into one of the most cheerful, happy, radiant Christians I have ever met. Thus, we can see that prayer will touch one with God's hand. He who rises from his prayer a better person has had his prayer answered.

"Whatever you ask in my name, I will do it." When God does it, it is a new creation made right and proper. "Old things are passed away; behold, all things are become new" (II Corinthians 5:17). Truly, God wants you to turn from the old life and into the new and good life. He wants to give you a new personality in His own image, beautified by His divine touch. Begin by following the cheerful, radiant thoughts and practices given to us by the Master.

However, remember your own strength will carry you only so far. You have to ask God to help you. Prayer will bring the good life. It enhances life. It lets us see the beauty of Jesus shining through. It gives strength for life. It transforms life. Ask God to help you. Prayer brings us close to God, helps us to know God, and to know what God is all about as He works with us in this world and the world to come.

"No eye has seen, nor ear heard, nor the heart of man conceived, what God has prepared for those who love him" (I Corinthians 2:9).

> Come, my soul, thy suit prepare:
> Jesus loves to answer prayer;
> He Himself has bid thee pray,
> Therefore will not say thee nay.
>
> —John Newton

If one is to live the good life and really "stay alive" as long as he lives, let him follow the techniques and thought pattern we have gleaned from the Master and outlined in these chapters. Then go to the Lord in prayer and ask for help. In asking God to help, *pray comprehensively;* that is, pray about all things. Pray *conversationally;* that is, let your prayer be the expression of your heart to God, and let God speak to you—a divine dialogue between you and your God. Pray *conditionally;* that is, pray as Christ prayed in Luke 22:42: "Not my will, but thine, be done."

On several occasions, I have heard Dr. Louis H. Evans, Sr. tell about attending a prayer meeting for a young mother suffering from polio. He reported that she had just come out of an iron lung after eight months and was sitting in a wheel chair. The doctor said she was hopelessly paralyzed. She had three little girls to rear. Several friends from the church were there at her side, and as they prayed, Dr. Evans said they besought the throne of grace as he had seldom heard, beseeching with travail and tears. He said that after this tremendous storming of the throne of God, the young mother began to pray: "O God, You know Your business better than I do. Of course, Lord, I would like to be well again and run and play with my children and kneel beside them as they say their prayers at eventide. I would rather they would not be ashamed of me, Lord. I would rather they could be proud of me, and I would love to walk and run with them once more. But God, as I said, You know Your business, and if I can best glorify You by being a cripple all my life, I am ready now, and dear God, I shall be happy, too. Amen."

Then, he said, it came, that quietness, that stillness, that happiness! He went on to say: "Ah, we all knew what *we* wanted, and we told God. She alone told God He could have what He wanted, and then came that peace and joy. Before they left the room, Dr. Evans said to her: "My dear, you have not been cured of polio, but you have conquered polio, and what a victory!"

Since that day the young mother has written a delightfully inspiring book through which she has been a splendid help and comfort to many people.

Have you problems, troubles, and difficulties that you cannot handle? Do you long to have a better life? Then put into practice these principles of our Lord and Master, Jesus Christ, and ask God to help you.

PRAYER: Almighty God, good and personal Father, I come to Thee with all things about which I am concerned. I speak to Thee; I call upon Thee; I listen to hear Thee answer in whatever way You would choose to speak to me. I come to Thee with the desires of my heart; dear God, knowing that You know your business better than I do, I finally cry, "Not my will but Thine be done." In the Master's name I pray. Amen.

HOW TO STAY ALIVE
ALL YOUR LIFE

by C. W. FRANKE

- Refreshing and invigorating to the secret of living the life of true freedom
- Beamed at the average church member who wants to know the joy of the full-orbed Christian life
- Shows the Christian how and why he should enjoy life more than anyone else
- Speaks to everyone in almost every situation in life
- Appeals to the unbeliever by showing him that the Christian life is not dull habit but dynamic hilarity
- Offers a rare combination of insight, humor, and apt illustration which reaches the reader "right where he lives"

For the person in search of faith, these chapters will provide loving, cheerful and tender admonition, solidly presenting the time-honored message of God and His redemptive work in the world.

For the person interested in psychology, chapters on the mind, imagination, and positive suggestion will attract and inform.

For the one looking for the more abundant life, chapters on "Life's Best Road," "Love," "Good Cheer," "Thanksgiving" and "Character" will be particularly apt.

For the downhearted, the chapters on "Self-doubt," "Bad Moods," "Fear," "Weakness" and "Worry" will be enlightening.

The fearful will find a helpful message in the chapters on "Procrastination," "Beauty," and "There Is No Wrong Side of Sixty."

[*continued on back flap*]

No. 9629